ENCHANTED EARTH

THE ROAD TO E...

Gillian England

MYSTIC HEALING THERAPIES

BOOK ONE

Copyright Gillian England 2023

ENCHANTED EARTH

TABLE OF CONTENTS

Chapter 1 With Us 4
Chapter 2 A Different Reality 15
Chapter 3 Souls with a Purpose 29
Chapter 4 More to Come 38
Chapter 5 Finding Self 51
Chapter 6 A Mirror View 66

Gillian England

MYSTIC HEALING THERAPIES

BOOK ONE

INTRODUCTION

This is a unique story about a different reality, the tale of a being from a planet trillions of miles away in a different galaxy, and how this being manages the task it has been assigned, of assisting the developing consciousness of the human race. The story spans millions of years from the early days of sentient habitation on planet Earth, but is not about scientific facts as viewed from the current paradigm; rather an enchanted Earth.

The reader is taken on numerous fascinating journeys, getting tantalising glimpses into the secrets of creation, energy systems, the Akashic halls of knowledge, as well as spiritual phenomena such as astral travel, and reincarnation. Along the way, we meet enchanted creatures such as dragons, unicorns, pixies and tree spirits, gaining insights into their existence, and purpose.

As well as planet Earth, we hear about the main character's home planet, Rycia, many light years away. We are introduced to concepts of other realities and life forms existing on other planets, viewing reality from a very different perspective, celebrating diversity and otherness.

We invite you on this journey, attune to the deepest recesses of your memory and sub-conscious, open your mind to the wonderful, diverse lifeforms that used to live so freely and joyfully in our communities, you might be surprised where your journey may lead you.

Gillian England

CHAPTER 1 – WITH US

My natural homeland was many galaxies away, on the planet of Rycia, an unimaginable distance away, and by Earthly standards, my homeland was inconceivably ancient. Rycia was a planet roughly three or four times larger than planet Earth, many light years away. It had two main light Sources, or as you might say suns, and a number of satellites (moons). It was an energy centre, one of its tasks in its galaxy was to emit a loving vibration, and to direct the energy from this planet to other planets that were currently in the stages of development.

The energy Rycia forecasted, helped to lighten up and increase the vibrational level of the evolving planets. One of my main tasks on Rycia was to assist in the direction of this energy. I had leadership responsibilities. I felt blessed and honoured to be part of this civilisation, Rycia was very dear to me as this was where I first took consciousness in form after leaving the Source.

Things had not always been so tranquil and easy for Rycia's inhabitants. Just like planet Earth, we too had spent countless cycles of evolution learning to live with each other. Learning to live in harmony with the planet, and in our case, learning to respect and honour other cosmic influences, not just others on our planet, but others from our neighbouring planets.

We viewed visiting entities from other planets as guests, and as such we welcomed them to observe our way of life, and we liked to hear about their homelands and ways of living too. We communicated telepathically, there were no language barriers. We all learned from our differences, I marvelled at the divine life force and the scope for uniqueness and diversity across the galaxies and universes.

Very occasionally, we met with hostile visitors that may have the intent of taking from us without consent. However since we became an enlightened planet this was not a problem for us. If we felt under threat of attack, all it took was the collective energy of the Rycia inhabitants to purposely and consciously project loving thoughts. This created a mass of loving energy that acted like a psychic shield. The vibrational energy of this was so high it was impossible for any hostile visitors to penetrate it, as to be hostile meant their energy was operating at a lower vibrational level to ours. Just how sunshine will burn off any morning mist, our loving energy would see off any hostile force. Love really did conquer all. Before we became enlightened we were much more vulnerable to attack and invasion, as we had not yet learned that our greatest defence was the collective of loving energy.

In the early days of Rycia, in some respects, from a spiritual stance, we lead lives not too dis-similar to humans. We too fell into the traps of selfishness, greed and ego-driven power behaviours. We had not yet learned that these traits only lead us as individuals to further unhappiness, and as a collective, they only lead to disharmony in our communities and disruption to the inner core of our planet.

It took many years; time inconceivable for us to work out that the key to freedom was to give love and service to all. Slowly and gradually after many incarnations some of us began to realise this, and this paved the way for the remainder of the civilisation. The more of us that came to that realisation, the easier it became for the rest, they were being guided by good examples, also the collective consciousness was gaining momentum and helping others to see the light. Those surrounding us in our communities affected us. If most other people around us were loving and helpful, it was more likely that we ourselves would develop these traits, in this way our collective levels of consciousness increased in vibrational level, and we all became enlightened.

We had lived in a state of loving consciousness for eons of time, through acts of universal kindness and by performing loving deeds. All of Rycia's inhabitants had earned the right to move into a different sphere of existence should they choose. However many had chosen to stay with Rycia and use the collective power to direct this loving energy to other planets. Because all of the inhabitants of Rycia were enlightened it was a very "easy" place to live, literally everyone we came into contact with met us with love and respect, there was no crime, no discord, no unhappiness, it really was an ideal existence.

I had a soul group of beings that I was very close to, between us we'd had many incarnations together in varying roles. As beings we were not gender-specific, in other words we had both the male and female energies, but we didn't subscribe to a gender or have varying lives subscribed to such, we were just beings. To describe our appearance, we did not resemble the human Earthly form. We were tall, average height would be around three meters, the closest thing to compare to in Earthly terms would be a large bird-like, winged creature; we had facial features again not unlike a bird, we had golden coloured feather-like down. We had individual physical characteristics, though at that point in our evolution, the main distinguishing factors were our individual essence, we were able to tune into each other's essence easily. As individuals we respected each-others privacy, but beyond that we could see right through everyone, in terms of their thinking processes, essence and spiritual intent. There were no secrets, communication was rather simple, we just had to tune in to each-other and observe

I had delighted in this existence for millions of years of Earth time, but then my soul had got restless, I was looking for a new project where I would be able to express this universal love, and where I would be able to put to use the knowledge gained from my time spent on Rycia.

I requested an appointment with my elders, explained my desire to help the universes, and asked for their guidance and counsel. I was told that the conditions were becoming favourable for a new planet. The new planet would be positioned in a unique place in the galaxy, giving rise to potential diversity of form un-paralleled. They told me that the position in the galaxy coupled with the natural portholes of the planet would allow the emerging form consciousness to be influenced by a whole host of galactic influences, a true convergence of universal energies. I listened carefully to what my elders had to say, with each word my enthusiasm and desire to help growing in intensity; I could feel the energy bubbling up inside my heart. But would they allow me to be part of such a responsible task overseeing the birth and development of a new planet – planet Earth?

On Rycia, everyone on my vibrational level could see everyone else's inner-essence; my elders could also see the essence of their peers and the lower levels of vibration. However, I was unable to de-code some of the energy from the higher levels of vibration from the sphere of the elders. I would be able to given time, as long as I continued to grow and develop my soul, this could only be achieved by service. My plan was to assist the new planet Earth, in turn this would help my own development and move me towards greater integration with my elders, and my journey back to the Source.

A review meeting was held, the elders communicated with their own elders, since all was transparent, they were able to tune into my personal frequency and make their assessment as to my suitability for this task. They were able to access everything about me, all the good and bad deeds I'd done throughout the ages, throughout the individuality of my soul-essence. I quivered with anticipation, hoping that I'd done enough to qualify for that important task.

I watched this assessment, a bit like watching a movie but at super-speed. I too could see all my previous actions, they carefully reviewed how I had responded to difficulties and adversity in other life-times. Did I meet these challenges with love and dignity, or did I become defensive and angry? I could see that in the earlier times my responses tended to be driven by emotion and ego. However, as my soul developed, a gradual awakening was apparent, eventually over many life-times my reactions turned to responses, and I could see myself responding with love and wisdom as opposed to anger and defensiveness.

I could also observe that in my previous existences I'd been assigned various tasks which appeared to have had the purpose of testing me, almost as if the current task was always a possibility, and many of my former life-times were designed as a precursor to this, giving me opportunities to test my resilience. Taking me to the brink of my capabilities, seeing if I would cope with the most challenging situations. I took a moment to marvel at this, how the divine plan was so intricate, and how each life-time or existence was like a piece of a jigsaw, in time revealing a full picture, so inconceivably intelligent and marvellous.

Eventually I was told that I met the requirements for the new task; I was delighted, determined and committed to my task, but also a little awe-struck. Would I be able to cope with this? I referred back to the review movie, and literally reminded myself of all the preparatory incarnations, steadied myself, I was ready.

I was summoned to a planning meeting, I was told that others had also been subscribed to the task, though predominantly we would be working as individuals, rather than in teams, though at varying times throughout our incarnations we would have the opportunity to meet, especially at times when our combined energies would be required. At the planning meeting I was subject to an inter-active process, where the elders taught me about planet Earth, and what I could expect to find during my time there, along with suggestions on what I could do to help me adapt to the conditions of that planet. As a being from Rycia I was familiar with visiting a range of different planets, but most of these had been established, fully functioning planets.

Earth would be different as it would be a brand new planet. I was shown the blue-print of the planet, and could see the varying potentials of forms and civilisations. The thing that struck me most was the potential diversity of beings, animals, plants, landscapes and levels of spiritual consciousness.

My home planet of Rycia was no-where near as diverse; in fact no-where I had ever visited demonstrated as much diversity as this potential. What a wonderful place this planet Earth would be. I was told that what I was seeing were the potentials, and it would be the developing consciousness of the individual life-forms on the planet that would ultimately shape the outcome of the potential. I asked them to explain this further. They told me that there was no pre-determined "destiny" and that eventually some of the beings of the planet would be given free-will, and the choices they made would impact on all of the other life-forms of the planet.

They explained to me that for the beings given free-will, it would be a chance for them to develop their sense of responsibility for those that didn't have free will. They said that it was likely that a race known as humans would be given free-will, and that other existences such as elementals, animals, plants, crystals, trees would not. I pondered this, and thought to myself it seemed quite generous that the human race would have such influence on the potentiality of the planet, I hoped they would be wise.

They then told me that others from the team had been subscribed to non-human races and life forms, but that my particular task was to over-see the development of the human consciousness. This would mean I would take human incarnations and live with humanity. This way I would be subject to all the human foibles, enabling me to develop true empathy for the people I was serving. I briefly thought about my journey as a being from Rycia, and the bumps and scrapes I'd got myself into whilst I worked out how to apply my free will without using or misusing others, or in other words whilst I was transcending my free-will. I hoped as a human I would not make so much hard work of it! My elders picked up on my thoughts and told me that in a human incarnation I would be the same as everyone else insomuch as I would be subject to the natural laws of being human, so in a way I would need to go through the whole process of transcending free-will as a human all over again, even though I'd taken eons of Earth time to achieve this on my home land, Rycia.

I was shown outlines and possibilities for the potential evolution of the planet, through various categories of "time". On Rycia the concept of time was all encompassing, comprising of different time-zones existing simultaneously. I was told that on planet Earth time would be perceived in a much simpler linear fashion, with a perception that there would be a distinct difference from past, present and future. This was a new concept for me, so I made a point of studying it in more detail to prepare me for my lives on Earth. Another thing I was told I would need to adjust to was the density of physical matter on Earth. They told me that I would have to learn the natural laws of the planet, in order to be able to manifest matter using thought forms or sound.

On Rycia we had done this quite naturally, if we wished to manifest something, such as a building or landscape, all we needed to do was concentrate on the detail of what we wished to create, and it would manifest with relative ease. The only factor in this was that we would have needed to have accumulated enough "creation credits". We did this by generating loving kindness and service to others. It would be much more difficult on Earth, the elemental masters had the task of creating landscapes and nature, although from a free-will point of view there was the potential for the human race to interfere with this. Again it struck me how much power the humans would have to influence their world. I felt optimistic that they would be sensible to the divine plan.

In terms of manifesting buildings and physical objects, a period of thought evolution was likely to take place, where the human race would not be able to use thoughts to move matter, but would need to learn to physically manipulate matter, and have to build things with their hands. Again this was a new concept for me, so I studied it in detail. The elders informed me that during the transition process, as a human I was going to have to develop some patience, as things would not be instantly created on Earth.

They also informed me that humans were likely to go through a period of their development where it would not be possible to decipher another being's essence very easily. Humans would be able project an image or verbalise one point of view, but deep down in their reality mean a totally different thing.

It would be very difficult to judge the truth. I was told that this would allow humans the capacity to work through and transcend the temptation to deceive; this was another learning point for me, as on Rycia it was impossible to deceive anyone.

I was told about the possibilities for arts and music, apparently the human race would have great potential to develop these and express themselves through these mediums. Whilst on vacation from Rycia I had visited the great halls of music and arts on the astral planes. Since my soul was developed enough to reach these realms, I had witnessed the truly sublime works of these places. I was excited to think that planet Earth would have the potential to manifest and develop arts and music. I had visited many planets where the races had not chosen to develop these, this had given me a sense of lack and emptiness, as though they were missing out on beauty and the richness of being. I very much hoped that the human race would embrace the arts and music, and was looking forward to experiencing how the human consciousness would express themselves in these forms.

I was aware of how much the concept of imagination was a tangible phenomenon on Rycia, we used our imagination to create physical form (though a different physicality to Earth). I realised that on planet Earth, a human's imagination would be a less tangible concept, ideas conjured up in an imagination would most probably stay there. As I realised that transforming thought forms from the imagination to physical matter would take considerable skill and craftsmanship. It seemed strange to me that on Rycia imagination was such a fundamental part of our everyday existence, yet on Earth it would be viewed almost as fanciful or secondary on some level.

They wanted to ensure I was fully prepared for my assignment. The next thing I had to learn about was a concept of transport. On Rycia if we wished to visit another area of the planet, or visit a particular friend or relative all we had to do was set our intention to that place, imagine it, and we would instantly be there. I was told that on Earth during the stages of evolution the laws of matter would apply, I would physically have to move from one place to another, apparently thinking of a place would only take my mind, not my physical body. This would take some adaptation; no wonder the elders keep reminding me about patience!

The elders went on to explain planet Earth would be an excellent place for beings to develop and accumulate spiritual knowledge, and had the potential to be a true place of learning and development for all inhabitants of the planet. It was explained that eternal progress really was open to every soul, the process was eternal and all inclusive, progression and ultimate freedom of spirit was available for everyone. I was told it was not exclusive to some chosen race or dependant on subscription to a particular doctrine or religion; all we had to do was open our hearts to others, live in peace within our own sphere of existence, and as far as possible build peaceful relationships with all whom we come into contact with. Planet Earth would provide a suitable environment for all living beings to undertake lessons in spirit, love and progression, like a classroom of life.

They explained to me the human processes of birth, death and re-birth. That all humans, me included, would be subject to this. Basically prior to taking a human incarnation a soul would consult with its guides and the life- planners and decide what lessons it wished to learn and what attributes it wished to develop in that particular life-time. This would largely be dependent on the laws of karma. For a soul to be born into so called favourable conditions it would need to have accumulated the right karmic conditions for this in previous life-times. It would do this by service to others, or selfless acts of kindness. On the other hand, if in previous lives it had been selfish, greedy or unkind, then its karma might suggest that it experiences a life on the receiving end of this, to give it the opportunity to learn about the impact of such behaviours.

Enlightened souls that had already worked through and transcended free- will may choose to take an incarnation specifically designed for service to others or humanity. Their karmic laws would be slightly different and may have more choices in terms of their incarnation and the aspects surrounding this. Often these souls chose to be born into extremely difficult circumstances. For example they might opt for a birth into a family that historically had experienced relational problems for many generations, each new generation passing on the maladaptive behaviours and thinking processes. By incarnating into a troubled family such as this, the enlightened soul may be able to use their influence within the family to break the unhelpful patterns and cycles of a family's conditioned behaviours.

Although advanced, these souls could experience these life-times of service as extremely lonely and alien. Some of these souls would question themselves and believe their current conditions were due to "bad karma" as though they were paying off some terrible debt. But in reality these souls had chosen to incarnate as acts of service. If these souls were able to access their higher consciousness, and tune into the real purpose of their life, then they would find their acts of service a whole lot easier to bear.

Prior to birth the soul would be assigned a main spirit guide, sometimes known as a door-keeper or guardian angel. This spirit guide would be with the soul from the moment of birth, right through to death and beyond. They would help guide the soul, but would not act on their behalf, as they knew the importance of the soul learning the lessons for themselves. Prior to birth the soul and the guide would consult the life plan, seeing how ideally the soul would like to develop. However, it would not be a predetermined "destiny" rather a sketch of the main content and themes of the life it wished to lead. This would be imprinted on the higher-self and higher-consciousness of the soul, but at birth and upon entering human life, this would be forgotten by the day to day consciousness.

Humans could access knowledge from their higher-self by listening carefully to their inner voice, inner conscience or sense of "right and wrong". Some accessed this by sitting quietly or meditating, taking time to sit in nature, or simply by attuning themselves to the here and now, observing the present moment. There would be periods in history where humans would be more attuned to their natural state of mind and the higher-self. There was also potential for humans to become disconnected from their higher selves and spiritual purpose, it would be at those times that humanity would face its most fundamental challenges.

At the end of each incarnation, shortly after death when back in the spirit world, the individual would have the opportunity to meet with their spirit guide, and review the life they had just lead. During the life review the individual would appraise his or her actions, being able to see the spiritual value of the life lead. The mistakes and achievements would all be clear to see, there was no hiding from the truth. When one had wondered far from the intended life-plan this could be a difficult process to engage with, but on the other hand, lives that had been valuable in terms of service to others were recognised and the individual would see they had accumulated spiritual merit, which would be of great value for their soul going forward. From this stance any material "success" or any notion of "fame" or "celebrity" were seen as irrelevant, it was only acts of kindness and actions serving others that held any kind of credit or value.

I was reminded that living a human life was not easy. The laws of matter, the physicality of the planet, coupled with the inherent free-will all lead to potentials for mistakes. It would be easy to enter a human incarnation filled with good intent and hold high expectations of self for what could be achieved in that life time. However, once in the physicality of matter, leading an authentic spiritual life would likely feel a lot more challenging, than what was perhaps anticipated at the planning stage, whilst in the relatively comfortable realm of the spirit world.

Other factors would come into play, such as the stage of spiritual development of the planet herself and all its inhabitants, coupled with the local and global collective consciousness of other humans. There would always be the temptation to seek personal power and try to manipulate others. The male/female duality may lead to individuals feeling incomplete on some levels. The natural cycles of birth, aging and death could cause physical pain and mental suffering, especially if not understood fully with regard to the cause and effect of karma, within a spiritual and eternal context.

However demanding the Earthly conditions were, it was a perfect testing ground for humans to try out behaviours and learn the consequences of them. Apparently there was no-where quite as exacting as a physical incarnation on Earth to bring home certain lessons. Perhaps because when a soul was encased with a physical body it was extremely difficult to escape anywhere, so humans were forced to face up to their learning.

As I took part in this interactive learning process to prepare me for my journey to planet Earth, part of me felt eager and optimistic, but another part of me was very much in touch with the reality of the potential pitfalls and how difficult living a human life encased with matter might be. I consciously integrated all this information to my being, and prepared myself for the next stage of my existence as an incarnate of planet Earth.

We held a ceremony on Rycia, which was a blessing for all the Rycian inhabitants who had volunteered their services on Earth. We also sent blessings and positive energy for the in-coming new planet Earth and all her future inhabitants, this was a truly joyful and positive occasion. By collectively sending out positive energy from Rycia to planet Earth we were setting up psychic energy pathways, we knew this would be helpful for times to come. As each time any positive energy was sent to planet Earth, it would strengthen and reinforce the pathways, making the link energetically much stronger. Then once the Rycians took incarnations on Earth and mindfully connected Earth to Rycia, again this would reinforce all the energy work we had done in a two-way traffic sort of way.

My intuition told me that it would be many eons before my Earthly task would be completed; I said a fond farewell to my soul group, knowing that our meetings during these times would be fleeting and sporadic. But we were all happy to be of service to the Great Spirit, no matter what that reality would bring. As I made my way through the universe I took the opportunity to spread loving energy from my heart as I went along, just as an aeroplane leaves a vapour trail, I was leaving a trail of love and light as I travelled through the galaxies. I knew that the other Rycian's would be doing the same as they took their own journeys to their various assignments, it felt good to be doing something useful for the cosmos.

CHAPTER 2 – A DIFFERENT REALITY

BIRTH

Energies of unparalleled intensity were gathering, I watched and waited in the time before time, with total optimism and love, all was well. As the light and love fused to cataclysmic proportions, with an accumulation of everything good, mother Earth was born. I witnessed the total euphoria as the light energy birthed and synthesised with the physicality that became planet Earth. Born from pure love, every atom became. Pure mother, unspoilt, untouched. I basked in the virgin moment, and celebrated a new time/space/place awaiting the work.

Mother Earth yawned and consciousness dawned, there was no hurry, a minute could last ten thousand years. Gradually particles of the consciousness awoke and began to take forms, encased in versions of physical matter of a much finer and lighter vibration, pure, uncontaminated.

A beautiful time, when all existences beat to the same rhythm of life, contained in the knowledge that we were all derived from the same divine life- force, the Source. A time when living in unity and harmony with all others was as natural as taking a breath or turning to the sunshine. A time when all life- forms would communicate with each other, sometimes telepathically, other times simply by sharing a space side by side.

We were united with our differences of species, because as a collective of living organisms it had not occurred to us to observe differences. From our stand-point we were all inhabiting the same planet, and were all derived from the same Source, this naturally lead us to a feeling of connectedness with all that was. Holding respect, love and compassion for all other beings was a natural and integral part of everyday life.

Initially my consciousness took the forms of simple celled organisms, this was to ease me into Earth conditions gently, and also it served as an experiment in creation. Since my consciousness was relatively advanced, it served the purpose of allowing the creators a snap-shot of how these simple celled organisms might develop given time. My presence in these incarnations acted as a catalyst, the cell evolution accelerated by my presence. All living organisms were reliant on an in-coming consciousness of life-force, and would evolve dependant on the developing consciousness of that particular species.

Gradually the forms in which I incarnated evolved, during this process my higher-self was aware of what was happening, though I was passive as to what forms were chosen for me to "try out", I had offered my service, and I trusted in the knowledge and skills of the creators, I was happy to be of help.

At this point I was very much aware of, and in tune with the energy vibration of mother Earth. Being in passive states as simple organisms gave me the scope to merge with the very essence of the Earth, and get a real feel for her character. I could sense that mother Earth had warrior-like qualities, she was strong and vibrant, on the other hand she was gentle and forgiving. This seemed to me like the perfect balance. I felt fortunate to be on this assignment, and made efforts to tune in and communicate with mother Earth, to gain a better understanding of how I could best serve her, and the in-coming inhabitants.

At that time there did not seem to be much demarcation between the emerging species or mother Earth herself, it was as though we thought and acted as one. I wanted to learn about the different kingdoms of life; animal, vegetable and mineral, so I was granted numerous incarnations and in-sights into each of these domains to experience these forms of life. I will now give some accounts of my experiences of these at that point in Earth evolution. I invite you to put any pre-conceptions about previous inhabitation of life on Earth aside, and be open to different concepts of reality, because viewed from today's paradigm this may appear simply impossible!

One of my favourite incarnations during the early times was one of a dragon type creature. My wing-span would have been around thirty metres, I was covered in red and black scales, had a tail that extended about five metres and I had the gift of fire. I loved my ability to fly, and since the energy of the planet was of a much finer vibration, was able to travel vast distances across the planet at speed, so fast in fact that it didn't seem so much different to the speed of thought-travel I was used to on Rycia. There were other dragons incarnated at this time, of differing colours, green blue and purple. My main task was to assist the mineral masters in their creations, and also help communities solve disputes. If a situation arose which made conflict arise, then I may be called upon to act as a mediator to help bring about peace.

Let me tell you about the communities I served as a dragon. At this juncture of Earth evolution the main incarnates of the planet were elementals.

The elementals reflected the elements of fire, air, water and Earth. Each elemental being was derived from the particular element they represented. For example, the Earth elements were akin to the Earth, their qualities were very grounded, steady and sensible, being practical they were able to craft beautiful garments and objects from the raw materials of the Earth.

Examples of Earth elements at this time would be elf, inner-Earth and gnome like creatures. Their consciousness in form was relatively new, and in many ways they held the beauty and innocence of children, so inevitably there were quarrels and disagreements during the process of them learning about sharing space and relationships with others. If communities were unable to resolve their own issues, they would call upon the dragons to come and help. Often my work here was just enabling each party to see the situation from the opposing party's perspective. Even during conflicts, each party still held an underlying respect for each other. Most of the time these communities were simply stuck, they did not wish any harm to the other party, they simply needed guidance to find an amicable solution. All the elemental beings had a natural respect for each other, there was a true brotherhood and sisterhood prevalent throughout the world.

As a dragon, my residing place was the inner-Earth, often beneath mountains. I felt fortunate to share this space with the mineral kingdom. Each separate mountain range would have its own mineral master that would preside over that particular space. At this time the mineral masters would be a bit like alchemists, they were experimenting with the varying mineral and chemical elements of the Earth, and would try out mixing specific combinations of these, to produce exquisite crystals and jewels. I assisted them by using my gift of fire; and my personal vibrational level enabled the crystals to be charged with high frequency energy. I noted that even if the same basic elements went into the crystals, if a slightly different pressure or temperature of fire was applied, or a different thought-energy was present during the assembly process, then a unique product would be produced.

You may recognise the mineral masters as wizards, but I prefer to call them mineral masters as that reflects their purpose more accurately. The mineral masters could set the specific intention for every crystal. For example if they wanted to create a crystal designed specifically for healing energies, then healing thought-energy would be imbued into this, which would result in each crystal and jewel having its own individual qualities and consciousness. Sometimes if I was called to assist a dispute, the mineral masters would gift a crystal or jewel for me to take to the community that was experiencing difficulties. They would chose a crystal that would reflect the qualities of the need, and the crystal would assist in re-balancing the energies of the community. The communities I served were very respectful of the crystal energies, they would honour the crystals and would continue to ask the crystals for guidance, when I was no longer there to help. The mineral masters would be very careful to match up the qualities of the crystals to that of the community it was destined to serve.

Although these crystals and jewels were exquisitely beautiful and aesthetically marvellous, the elemental communities esteemed them primarily for their innate energies and true essence. Their outer beauty was secondary. At these times collecting jewels simply because they looked nice or for an "investment" was inconceivable, and would have been deemed extremely dis- respectful too. Since there was no monetary system or ideas of ownership, crystals and jewels took their rightful place in the world, as beautiful beings and holders of loving and wise energies. The mineral masters wished to assist the developing planet by producing crystals and jewels that would encapsulate a plethora of loving and wise energies that were inherent qualities of the mineral masters themselves.

For countless millennia, the inhabiting species understood the divine laws and purpose of crystals, and received much comfort and guidance from them. It was not until later on in the cycle of Earth existences that the dominant inhabiting species of the times began to misuse the powers inherent in the crystals. After which, as part of the cleansing process, sadly much of the magical knowledge of the crystals was lost to the vast majority of Earth inhabitants.

My home at this particular time was in a labyrinth of caves, huge caverns beneath a range of mountains; the caverns took on mountainous proportions of indescribable beauty that stretched out almost as far as the mountain range itself. There were different sections and underground rooms, each one having slightly different mineral components and energies, almost like huge natural laboratories, where the resident mineral master worked and created. There was no daylight in the caverns, but there were certain rocks that emitted a gentle and pleasing light, so day light was not necessary, there was a calm and peaceful atmosphere throughout.

I will call the mineral master/wizard in this case Bob (though this was not his real name). Bob was my companion and I considered him to be a friend, he took on a humanoid appearance, was around two meters in height, with a very slim and slight frame. He spent his entire time inside the caverns creating. He did not see day light or any sunshine, therefore his skin took on an almost translucent appearance. He had large eyes, very pale in colour, he had a few wisps of thin whitish hair, but mostly the body was hairless. His appearance was quite typical of the inner-Earth beings at that time. Although I've referred to Bob as being male gender, it would be more accurate to say he was a-sexual, he did not recognise or pursue sexuality, he was completely committed to his task of creation. Bob was a very gentle and loving being, yet he did not appear to have a need for companionship or relationships. Although I enjoyed his company and presence very much, I suspected he saw me simply in terms of how I might assist him to serve the planet, rather than viewing me in relational terms of a companion. I observed this to be the case for most of the inner- Earth masters, steadfast, loving and wise, perfectly self-contained in their work.

Almost all the other caverns had a dragon subscribed to them. Sometimes if Bob discovered an important mineral combination; he would task me to let the other mineral masters know about it. In reality we could have telepathically communicated these new discoveries, but it was really good to mix and socialise with the other dragons, many of whom were descendants of Rycia and other enlightened planets. Sometimes as souls, we dragons might recognise each other from our previous incarnations on other planets. Although this was observed, we did not speak of it, as it was felt that we needed to focus on our current lives and tasks. However our shared history made for a very pleasant and fulfilling time when we did meet, and in some ways made those early days of being separated from our mother planets easier to cope with, therefore we were allowed this indulgence.

Now I will give you an example of the communities I served and a dispute that would have been typical of the one I would be called to assist with. When my assistance was required the head of the community would send a telepathic signal that help was required. This would come to me like a picture in my mind, I would then tune in and focus my attention on the request, taking in all the relevant factors and information from the community elder. I would then consult with Bob and we would determine a possible way forward, considering any crystals or jewels that may benefit the community energy. With an action plan in place, I would leave the cavern and journey to find the community. I would receive an impression of the place I was looking for and would intuitively find the right place.

Flying around the untouched virgin landscapes of planet Earth, I must have portrayed a magnificent and impressive silhouette, as much excitement was generated when I landed. The communities at this time held the dragons in very high regard, viewing them as being a bit like gods. The thinking processes of the people on Earth at these times were very different to what they are today, they accepted and welcomed people from other realms and species. Life for everyone was far more multi-dimensional. However, the people were quite shy in my presence; the youngsters would often hide behind the more confident characters, sneaking a peek of me when they thought I would not notice. It was no wonder they viewed me with a degree of caution, as compared to them I was huge in stature. The people I am referring to took on elf and gnome-like appearances. The gnomes were around eighty five centimetres to a metre tall with a stocky appearance, elves tended to be taller and slimmer built, between one meter sixty to one meter eighty tall. The most striking thing about them all were their bright shining eyes, they all had beautiful twinkling, almost crystal-like eyes that were rather mesmerising. There is a saying that " the eyes are the window to the soul" if that was the case then, the gnomes and elves eyes perfectly reflected the beauty of the souls incarnated at those times, beautiful, clear, bright, untouched.

Almost always with very few exceptions they were beautifully attired in hand-stitched garments, crafted to the highest standards. Red green and brown were their favourite colours; the males would wear breeches, shirts and waist coats, the females tunics or smocks. Their shoes would be made from a
fibrous material crafted from tree bark, everything was derived from the raw materials of the Earth, as during these times it would have been incomprehensible to take the life of another being to use their skin or flesh for clothing or food. Every life form was held in respect, so even though tree bark was obtained for making shoes, before taking the bark, the gnomes and elves would ask the tree spirit for permission to take the bark, and would liaise with the tree as to how best to harvest the product, to ensure the least impact for the tree.

Tree and plant material would only be used with the blessings of the plant and tree spirits. When a material was utilised, the gnomes and elves would give thanks to the nature spirits for proving the resource. It was a community existence based completely on love and respect, every action undertaken would be considered in the context of everyone else. The concept of "me and mine" were alien. All life-forms understood the unity and connectedness of sharing the physical plane of planet Earth, there was no "dominant species". The time before time, prior to human incarnation on the planet. As such, the elemental people were very open hearted and trusting, deceit, distrust and defence mechanisms were unknown phenomena.

More often than not, gnomes would live in family groups, with a male and female as partners, and would have numerous off-spring. Typically their homes would be of a simple design, yet everything would be beautifully hand crafted, made with much love care and attention. There was no place for frippery, everything in the home served a utilitarian function, yet equally every functional item was a piece of art in itself. Preferred locations for their homes would be places of natural beauty, or where the Earth energy systems were particularly compatible. Places such as woodland dells, waterfalls or hillsides were popular choices. Before setting up home, they would consult with the nature spirits of the locations, to ensure every being was in agreement with the proposed site, if for any reason the nature spirits objected then the elementals would listen to the alternative suggestions and more often than not would respectfully heed the advice. Very occasionally I would be called up to help resolve conflict in these areas. Another main Source of conflict would be regarding the making and breaking of partnership bonds. Gnomes and elves did not get married as such, but if they wished, they could pledge to be official partners, this was usual if they were planning a family. They were free to mutually extract themselves from the bond if they both wished, sometimes I might be called if one partner wished to end the bond, but the other did not. I may also be called upon to help, if for example there was more than one person wishing to bond with another.

To help resolve the community problems, I would call a meeting of all those involved, along with the family and community elders, we would all sit in a circle, and if crystals were to be used, they would be placed in the centre of the circle. The meeting would start with an invocation, asking that we all linked to the universal wisdom to help find a solution, then each party would be given opportunity to voice their own view. I would try to get the parties to see events from the opposing position. With some gentle guidance more often than not a solution would be found. The communities at this time were very loving and trusting, and rarely offered any opposition to the suggestions made. Once a solution had been found, we would offer thanks to the universe for its wisdom, before drawing the meeting to a close.

If they had been gifted crystals I would show the people where in their community to place the crystals for maximum energy benefit, and how to take care of them. This might involve chanting certain phrases, cleansing the crystals with spring water or smoke, or making offerings of certain herbs and plants. In all cases the crystals would be welcomed into the communities as honoured guests, the people holding respect, reverence and gratitude for the part the crystals played in their lives. The crystals would be passed down through the generations, and due to the respect and reverence held for them, over time these crystals would build up much power and energy. This was recognised by the communities, which in turn made the crystals even more respected and powerful, leading to the point in evolution where calling upon the dragons was no longer necessary, as the crystals themselves could do the work.

It was a truly beautiful time to be living life on planet Earth, and since the Earth vibration at this point was much lighter, there was less differentiation between the physical plane and the astral planes, the elemental world was multi-dimensional. Elemental beings were very easily able to visit the astral plains, and access other realities, whilst maintaining their Earthly stance. This would be the norm rather than the exception, though it has to be remembered that the natural laws of such planes of existences existed, and the elemental beings would only be permitted to visit the planes of existence that were compatible to their own vibrational energy level. Having the ability to visit other realities enhanced the feeling of inter-connectedness; beings understood that their particular race and culture was just one example of the many forms of life prolific throughout the universes.

I also took incarnations as tree and nature spirits, sometimes these are known as divas or faeries. In order for me to take on incarnations in the nature realms, I had to call upon all that was gentle and patient within my nature. Tree spirits gave a vital service regarding the well-being of the planet on both physical and non-physical levels. Physically they would convert carbon dioxide into oxygen, help to give structure to landscapes preventing natural erosion, and provide habitats for animals and insects, as well as providing vital materials for building and clothing. This was service enough, but on a non- physical level their contribution was fundamental to the vibrational level of the planet. As a tree spirit I learned about holding energy frequencies, my role was to be almost like a battery cell, or an energy holder. I was charged with a certain energy that was manifested in the physical form of a tree, my job was to simply and patiently stay in the location and maintain that energy vibration. All the other tree spirits were subscribed the same task, together we held a collective of wisdom and a steadfast energy that withstood cycles of time.

I will briefly describe a scene from a life spent as a willow tree in a woodland dell; the scent of the bluebell type flowers was heady, the brilliant green hue of the foliage surrounded us, intercepted by the vibrant colours of fragrant flowers. We were joining in communion, a place of coming together just for the purpose of coming together to blend our energies. It was a happy, joyous occasion, there was no agenda other than to blend and attune. As a collective we took on many different physical forms, ranging from the plant and tree spirit, to the fungi, light energy divas, insects, elementals, pixies, faeries, gnomes, salamander, wizards, unicorns, griffins, pegasus, dragons, to name but a few.

We knew our physical forms varied greatly from each other, this was not a problem for us, in fact we marvelled at each species' different forms, strengths and talents, the main thing was we knew we were all derived from the same Source, the divine life-force that is in every creation, we were truly united. A sense of peace prevailed; the emphasis on being, not doing, our purpose was to acclimatise to being incarnate on this relatively new planet Earth. Coming together like this enabled individuals to learn about the different domains of life, and about each other's task and purposes. For many it was their first incarnation in form since leaving the Source, so this communion was a vital step in recognising themselves as individual spirits. The contrasted variations of the physical forms in these communities assisted in this separation and identification of "self". It was interesting to consider that only by observing, appreciating differences, and engaging with others in the context of the diverse communities could individuals start to flourish and grow towards their own individual potential. I pondered this, and sensed that this would be a very important lesson for the developing races of planet Earth. At this time the vibrational energy of the planet was very light, so light that in fact, that physical manifestation was only just possible, the collective consciousness of all beings emitted peace and joy.

As a tree diva I observed communities form, live out their life-times, then move on to new dimensions/incarnations all whilst I was in the same incarnation. In many ways these long-lasting incarnations were very useful for me as a soul, because being tied to a specific place on planet Earth helped me to develop qualities of patience, observation and acceptance. This was not always easy for me, as I was used to taking a much more mobile and pragmatic approach to life, whereas being a tree spirit helped me to develop a degree of serenity.

I undertook a number of incarnations as faeries; these took a similar essence to tree divas but being more mobile I didn't have to be quite so patient. The Faerie race loved to have fun and play innocuous tricks on each other, they were much attuned to kindness and joy, if they spotted an individual that was behaving contra to joy and kindness, the faeries would like nothing more than to invent a plan that would help the "offender" realise that their behaviour was undesirable. This would be undertaken in a good natured kind of way, more often than not resulting in joy and kindness being restored, which in turn prevented a down-turn in the local energy, thus maintaining the integrity of the communities' vibrational frequency. At these times all beings recognised their part in keeping the vibrational well-being of their communities. They understood that by taking personal responsibility for their own personal energy vibration this would help maintain the community vibrational frequency. They also were aware that the community energies naturally joined as a collective to form the energy frequency of planet Earth. In view of this, individuals knew that every individual thought, word and deed would ultimately impact on the vibrational level of the entire planet.

During these times unicorns were in existence, most people are familiar with the image of a unicorn; these were magnificent creatures, resembling huge white horses, with a golden or silver horn extending from their forehead. Currently the unicorn horn is often portrayed as relatively short, when in reality the horn could easily extend four or five metres in height, and would be at least twice the height of the animal itself. They had beautiful shinning manes and tales, wing spans of around six meters; their fundamental characteristic was strength and gentleness. They were great ambassadors of the communities; their maxim was "solidarity". The true purpose of their long extended horns has been lost throughout the ages, and is little understood today. However, these were actually phenomenal vortexes of energy, which they used for healing and energy-balancing purposes. Should they encounter a situation where the energy levels had fallen, they could imbue the place with the energy from their horns, helping to keep the local vibration level intact. This was another example of the community endeavour to keep the collective energy at optimum levels.

Unicorns were exceptionally intuitive animals, and sought to offer help and assistance to anyone who was feeling out of sorts or not quite themselves. Anxiety and depression had not yet manifested at these times, but if a being was experiencing any internal discord, the unicorns could be called upon to assist. Their ability to fly enabled them to access the people who needed them the most. Just like with the dragons, if unicorns were called upon for help, a psychic message would be put out into the ether, and the unicorns would intuitively respond. It is fair to say that everyone loved the unicorns, they always received a warm welcome, and their very presence added a particular spark and essence to any gathering.

More often than not, unicorns were called upon by individuals to help solve personal problems; however, what unicorns specialised in was the ability to enable individuals to journey to other realms and planes of existence. They were very spiritually evolved beings and naturally held high frequency energy vibrations, and it was because of this they were able to access the many different spiritual planes of existence. Unicorns were particularly helpful to individuals who were pursuing spiritual quests, or quests for knowledge. Students wishing to expand their spiritual knowledge were able to accompany the unicorns to the varying realms. The students would not be able to access these realms by themselves because their energy vibrations were not evolved enough, but the unicorns were able to hold the energy frequency for these less evolved students. The destinations for these spiritual journeys would be determined by the students learning plans. There would always be a strong rationale and purpose for the journeying. It was viewed as a sacred service given by the unicorns, and in fact it took quite a lot of the unicorns' psychic energy, because they had to compensate for the lower energy vibrations of the student, whilst entering much higher frequency realms. The unicorns horns would help with the transfer and balance of energies, as they in themselves were a terrific holders of energy, almost like tremendously powerful batteries.

Lets now give an example of a unicorn journey, and how in this instance Blanch the unicorn offered his services to Manche the inner-Earth being. As stated previously inner-Earth beings were a-sexual, encompassing both sexes, but for the purpose of the story I will refer to Manche as a female and Blanch as male. Manche had taken an apprenticeship with the inner-Earth masters, and wished to understand more about the universe and the material composition of other planets. Along with her teachers, it was decided that a request would be sent to the unicorns, for a journey to the Halls of Knowledge. This was not decided lightly, but it was felt that Manche was showing great potential as a master herself, so the psychic request was sent out on the ether.

The request was picked up by the unicorn council, approved, and the wonderful, wise unicorn Blanch was delegated to undertake the task. Although inner-Earth beings had a reputation for being calm, collected and somewhat unemotional, there was most certainly an air of pleasant anticipation in respect of Manche's proposed journey to the Halls of Knowledge. Not least because the inner-Earth beings recognised this as being a privileged learning opportunity, and they were united in the support they felt for Manche and this wonderful chance she had been granted. Prior to coming together with Blanch, Manche had spent a lot of time in preparation. She had undertaken much inner-reflection work, and had also formulated salient questions and specific areas of learning that she wished to develop. She had also prepared herself spiritually for the quest, by consciously engaging in acts of love and service to others, and had psychically cleansed her energy system, as she knew that to get the most from this experience, she needed her own energy system to be operating on the highest vibrational level possible.

It was a joyous occasion when Blanch arrived at the inner-Earth dwelling place, the community joined together in wishing Manche a fulfilling and enlightening experience. Manche accepted the good wishes, before climbing onto Blanch's back, steadying herself by holding on to the unicorn's magnificent mane. They were ready to leave, Blanch unfolded his enormous pristine white feathered wings, then with a gentle nod of the head and a burst of twinkling energy they were off! Manche felt a whoosh of energy like a warm wind, she then felt a sensation of being propelled forwards, yet at the same time felt somehow as though she was going in on herself. All of her senses seemed to be energised and engaged on many different levels, it felt almost like an out of the body experience, yet on the other hand she felt in full awareness and consciousness of everything that was happening, as she journeyed on the back of the magnificent creature.

Manche had never felt so alive or at one with the universe, it was as though she was blending in with everything that ever was, a complete sense of belonging. It was easy for her to understand how we were all part of the divine life-force the Source. In a state of exhilaration and bliss, Manche arrived at the great Halls of Knowledge. It was difficult for her to comprehend the vastness, depth and potentials of the place. Existing on the etheric realms, operating on extremely high levels of vibration, the Halls of Knowledge contained records of all the intelligence and wisdom of the universe. Everything was categorised and divided into planetary sections, and sub-sections, and just as you have librarians and subject specialists in regular libraries on Earth, it was the same in the Halls of Knowledge, only on a scale of incomprehensible magnitude. When journeying to the Halls of Knowledge some may choose to conceptualise them as vast universities or learning centres, others may think of them as huge computer systems capable of storing infinite data, it would depend upon your worldly experience and internal frame of reference, as to how you might conceptualise them yourself.

Just as you may have security offices on duty at regular libraries or museums, there were guardians of knowledge for every section in the Halls of Knowledge. Accessibility was by appointment only, in order to be able to cope with the high vibrational energy, those from the less evolved realms (such as Manche from planet Earth), would need to be accompanied by a higher-being. Manche had Blanch to help sustain the energy levels, however she was also accompanied by her spirit guide and the higher beings akin to her own spirit guide. Manche and her entourage arrived at the appropriate place, she had explained her reasons for the visit and had put in a request before their arrival, so was granted entry straight away.

It was a poignant learning experience for all present; Manche was afforded great insight into the secrets and formulas of inner Earth. She learned the secrets of physical manifestation and manipulation of matter using sound energy and condensed thought processes. She learned about the thought processes and energies that are needed to manifest and create jewels, gems and minerals, as well as landscapes and weather systems. She also learned how thought energy can be used to manipulate matter in general; this was mainly imbued to her via the creators. For them to impart such knowledge they must have felt trust and confidence in her. Manche was well aware of this responsibility, she felt a little in awe but at the same time excited by her newfound insights. She was sure she would be able to use this knowledge to assist the development and evolution of planet Earth.

Once you have entered the Halls of Knowledge and have experienced the learning process, the lessons you learn will stay with you on some level for all of time. There may be incarnations where the information is not consciously accessible or times when it is dormant, but on a fundamental level the memory is permanent, it cannot be wiped out. In some ways being party to knowledge of this nature can be a big test in terms of a soul's free will. It might be tempting to use the knowledge for personal gain or power, or to lose sight of its sacredness. Accounts of black magic, and the story of the demise of Atlantis are examples of what can happen, should the knowledge be misused, disrespected, and asserted outside of the parameters of the Universal Law.

However, this was not Manche's path, she was going to use the knowledge for the good of all, not for personal gain. When she arrived back to her inner- Earth dwelling place, there was joy and celebration. The community gathered, and though Manche was naturally a little shy, she gave the community an account of her experience journeying to this other realm. Obviously much of what she had learnt was sacred knowledge, not to be shared in a public domain, but there was much she was able to share about many of the magical aspects of the journey itself, and of the wise and loving beings she had encountered.

Since the community had a great sense of connectedness, everyone felt a sense of awe and wonder in respect of Manche's experiences. They felt privileged that a member of their own community had been granted such an experience. They understood the interconnectedness of everyone and everything, and knew this was a benefit to them all, not just to Manche personally. It was truly uplifting on so many levels, since Manche had been exposed to the higher energy frequencies, she brought some of this high-energy back in her aura, which was translated into the collective community energy field, so as well as it being a joyful occasion for the community, it was also very positive from an energetic stance. During these times it was normal for people to observe psychic energy levels, so many people could consciously feel the local energy levels increase. This in itself brought a sense of connectedness, satisfaction and well-being.

As for Blanch, he had fulfilled his duty of assisting Manche on her epic journey, so after parting company he headed back to his homeland and prepared for his next assignment. As was the case for many beings present on the planet at that time, Blanch and the other unicorns dedicated their entire lives to helping others. This had a knock-on effect on the collective consciousness of the planet, as in many ways it was normal to be selfless, which in itself perpetuated others to be selfless and give a life of service. A truly wonderful chapter in Earth's history, however as the story shows, over time, the vibrational level of the Earth declined, conditions for unicorn habitation became unfavourable; their vortex energy horns could not manifest in the much denser conditions that prevailed on the Earth in later times, so sadly these magnificent animals lost their horns and wings, and became more horse- like in appearance. Unfortunately they were deemed mythical creatures of the imagination, instead of being seen as the supreme wise beings they truly are.

CHAPTER 3 – SOULS WITH A PURPOSE

The current view scientists' purport as being the age of sentient inhabitation of the planet is inaccurate, the Earth has sustained sentient life for far longer than can be conceived or measured with "modern day" science. The Earth has been through many cycles of development and has been home to many, many different species.

There are numerous reasons why it is almost impossible to find evidence of these earlier civilisations. Some of the previous civilisations have been so much at variance to current life, presently people would not know what to look for, they could pass an obvious clue to previous existences, but completely miss the evidence, as it would be so far removed from what they would expect to find.

Some of the previous cycles of physical existence operated on a much higher frequency of vibration, so just as we cannot physically see radio or microwaves, then like-wise we can literally be unable to tune into the frequency of the previous vibrations. Also there have been periods in Earth's development that have necessitated regeneration on a vast scale, almost like wiping the slate clean, or a "factory re-set" when the former civilisations have been totally lost and engulfed by mother Earth, in order to enable cleansing, healing and regeneration.

We go now to a time before time as we know it, when Earth was reaching a point where it was ready to enable beings with free-will to be incarnated. At this point, my form was vaguely human-like, most of the others in human-like forms at that time were also enlightened souls from other existences such as Rycia, that had volunteered to incarnate to act as the prototype for the human-like body, and offer feedback to the body elemental masters/creators with regard to any improvements that could be made to the human-like form. We were living largely in complete spiritual consciousness of our life-plans, this was very rewarding work. In terms of Earth time, this era of preparation spun millions of Earth years, but since we were comparing our perception of time to eternity, this seemed like a relatively short period. We were aware that once the refinements had been made to the physical forms, then it would be time for the new souls to incarnate on Earth, and begin their journey of transcending free-will. We prepared for this, and knew that once these new souls arrived, then the collective energy systems of the planet would change to accommodate their thought-forms, we were aware that the vibrational energy was likely to slow down a little and become denser.

The prototypes had been adjusted, there had been countless preparatory incarnations to ensure that the human body had all the necessary functions available, now the time had come for souls to be incarnated having been given full free-will to begin their Earth journeys incarnated into a physical body as fully conscious autonomous beings. In my life plan it had been decided that I would have two primary tasks, I would take the role of a mother and would also assist in the organisation of the community, and act as spiritual leader. These two roles would serve the function of producing off-spring with Rycian energy, that would be helpful in the maintenance of the energy system of our communities and a legacy for future generations. Acting as spiritual leader would give the brand-new communities some guidance and ideas of how they could organise themselves, and link with their higher-selves and other spiritual realms.

In terms of the mother role I was given a partner who was very much of the Earth's essence; our task was to breed and produce vehicles for the in-coming souls, it had been decided that my Rycian energy would be mixed with that of the Earth, so I was given a partner from planet Earth. My partner had a beautiful soul, he was gentle and had his own wisdom, he was extremely practical and "down to Earth", he found the physicality of Earth easy to negotiate, he was tenacious and competent, having the ability to craft and produce almost anything he wanted from the raw materials of the Earth. However my negotiation of matter was the pole opposite. I found the physicality of Earth very challenging, simple practical tasks such as sewing or dressing myself were difficult. My physical co-ordination was at times awkward, I was rather clumsy, I genuinely struggled with anything that involved using fine motor skills, yet I could easily fathom complex thinking strategies, had a highly attuned intuition, and could effortlessly foresee outcomes of future events.

My partner and I were so very different in essence that our life together was fraught with difficulties and misunderstandings. We seemed so much at variance with each other, if I said one thing, he would be thinking the opposite, if I was inclined to go one way, naturally he would be inclined to go the opposite way. We were like two doors, that swung in the opposite directions, our relationship was based on mutual respect, there was a strong physical attraction, (this was in the plan as our purpose was to breed), but we had to work extremely hard developing a loving relationship. We were literally from two different planets.

We spent much of our time arguing and feeling frustrated with one another, I would sometimes catch myself reminiscing over soul relationships I'd experienced before, and noted how far this relationship was from a soul connection. This could make me feel lonely and very much on my own, but then I connected to my higher-self, tuned in to see the bigger picture of my existence, which resulted in any feelings of frustration and loneliness being forgotten.

During this incarnation and life together we had thirteen children, I cannot say that I was a natural mother, I certainly did not enjoy the pregnancy condition, and although I loved and cared for all my children very much, I held my roles as mother and spiritual leader close to my heart in equal measure. It was as though I recognised that my mother role was to serve humanity by providing vehicles for life, rather than it being an innate need in my own being to produce so many children.

My position in the community was leader, I was literally first in command, this had come about so that I could use my higher Rycian knowledge to set up and organise the in-coming communities. It was as though the people at this time recognised that my essence was not of the Earth, and perhaps as a result of what they considered my advanced knowledge and foresight, that they seemed to esteem me as some sort of demi-god. I was indifferent to this perceived status, as countless incarnations on Rycia had helped prepare me to rise above any potential ego influences; I remained steadfast on my path, and would not allow inconveniences of power-trips or ego impede the task ascribed to me.

Very occasionally I would encounter situations where others wished to challenge my leadership position; on occasion there were also displays of jealousy regarding my perceived status. I would meet these challenges with love and openness; I would invite those challenging me to a meeting. Prior to the meeting I would tune into my higher-self, and attempt to gain a higher perspective on the issues at hand, I would always ask for guidance and assistance so that an amicable solution could be found. I would also infuse the situation with love and light, as I knew that this loving energy would ultimately resolve the issues. There were times when I asked permission to speak with the higher selves of the individuals involved; I would take that opportunity to connect with the soul energy of the individuals, and ask them how their current intentions were serving their life plan/purpose. These strategies were enough to resolve the issues. As a consequence, my position as spiritual/community leader never experienced any serious threats.

Conditions for life on Earth at that time were very favourable. Apart from the relationship with my partner, there was an air of calmness all around, the energy systems and weather patterns were very stable. The climate was temperate, we had a simple diet of nuts, leaves and berries, we were vegetarian, we would not kill or eat other creatures, to do this would have felt like killing our brothers and sisters. We lived in harmony with the other beings, paying our respects to all other life-forms with whom we shared the planet.

The human race at this time was largely calm and gentle, and in some ways had child-like qualities of innocence and trust. I loved my task of helping communities with structure and organisation, and showing them how to attune to their spiritual natures, different realms and dimensions. I did not encounter many difficulties with this, as mostly people were open to suggestion and were extremely compliant to my counsel, it was as though they weren't quite in touch with their free-will, and were looking for guidance as to how to conduct their lives.

In contrast, life at home was very challenging; my partner was very much in touch with his free-will and had no problem whatsoever asserting this against my wishes! I found this quite a culture shock, as I was used to people readily accepting my advice. Yet my partner and I were so very different, if given the same scenario, rarely would we reach the same conclusion. We naturally gravitated in opposite directions, I can honestly say that up until that point, my relationship with my partner was by far the biggest challenge I had faced since leaving Rycia.

I realised I was struggling to cope, my life felt problematic; I felt fed up and emotionally spent. I knew I needed help, and recognised I needed to get a spiritual perspective on the situation so I made a point of tuning into my inner/higher-self, and asking my spirit guides for guidance. They explained that my partner was helping me achieve balance in this incarnation, like the Yin/Yang dynamic, without his influence, I would not be able to find my equilibrium. Even though it felt difficult, it was the best thing for me as a soul. We had been placed together to help the polarities of the Earth dimension and the star dimension (in this case Rycia) to blend, incorporating Rycian energy would help maintain the energy frequency of the Earth, my partner was giving a great service to the Earth by breeding with me, from his point of view surely it would be much easier for him to have a partner also from the Earth, instead of trying to cope with my full-on Rycia energy and our stark differences. It was in our life-plans to be together, so far we had adhered to the scheme, I could also see that as well as breeding, our task was to learn to live together, in love and harmony despite our differences.

My guides told me that humanity was going to have to learn to live together in love and harmony whilst honouring the diversity and differences abundant on the planet. They said that this would start with my partner and I, saying that unless I could learn to do this successfully then I would not be equipped to help the developing races with their challenges of championing diversity. I recognised the value and wisdom in this advice, I felt gratitude to my guides for putting me back in touch with my life-plan. With this insight, and with my soul in control (rather than the emotional self), I returned to my partner in a much clearer and calmer frame of mind, we spent a pleasant evening together, and consciously conceived another child.

My first pregnancy was quite an ordeal; I was in many ways still adjusting to being incarnated as an Earth being, so when the Earth energy of my partner joined with me, and a child was created, I had to adjust to the energy of Earth being planted directly in my womb. I felt out of sorts for many weeks, not just with the usual pregnancy issues such as feeling nauseous and tired, but more to do with the altering vibration of my body. I was accommodating another soul's energy, and due to my developed levels of attunement, I felt this acutely. On the positive side, I could tell immediately when conception had taken place, so was able to take care of myself from the outset. I was also able to communicate with the in-coming soul of the baby, so was able to build a relationship with him right from the earliest times, telling him about life on Earth and our community, and also of my star heritage and life on Rycia. His soul had been hovering and waiting to join us, like all of our children, he had chosen to incarnate on Earth at these times with us as parents, in order to serve humanity and the in-coming civilisations.

I struggled on with my pregnancy, definitely not an "Earth mother!" At the time of my labour, I took to my chambers, it would have been usual for the women of the community to visit a woman in labour and bring gifts and encouragement. When word got around that I was entering labour, much excitement was generated. I was touched by this, and was honoured that others were excited to welcome another being into the world. Perhaps it was my heritage of being from Rycia, or the fact that I was looked upon as the head of the community, but I could not face having visitors, so chose to undertake my labour with a few trusted females, I hoped that this was not seen as a rejection of the people, but I felt the birth needed to be a private affair.

At the moment of birth, there was an intensely bright flash of silver-white light, followed by an enormous crash and bang sound in the delivery room, it was as though lightening had stuck in the very room. I immediately recognised that it was the soul of my baby having to reduce his natural soul frequency in order for him to be able to cope with the lower vibration on Earth, the excess of his energy resulted in it having to dissipate as lightening phenomena in the room. This soul had not been incarnated on Earth before, but was a very highly evolved soul from another planetary system (different from Rycia). I would be interested to see how he faired being in a human body, and I knew he would need a gentle environment to help his transition to these frequencies.

Word got around the community about the circumstances of our son's birth, the people celebrated, there was a genuine sense of joy, many brought simple gifts such as flowers or stones, others bestowed blessing, or sent nurturing and positive energy vibes. In those times people were much more accepting and accustomed to the concepts of others coming to Earth from different realms, they saw the lightening birth as a good omen, their hearts were open, and there was no sense of division or separateness. Perhaps it was due to my position as leader that the births of our children were looked upon as real milestones in the community; the births were celebrated perhaps as royal births are celebrated in current times. I would mention though, that our children would still run freely with all the other children in the community, there was no sense of superiority based on birth rights, that simply would not have occurred to anyone. It was a time before hierarchical systems, a time when anyone could become a community leader, the only qualification necessary was to have a loving open heart, an intention to tune into the higher wisdom of the universe and have the ability to bring that wisdom into the community.

All of our children were deeply loved; they were all so different and possessed their own individual talents and quirks. It was quickly apparent whether a child had predominantly inherited its mother's or father's ways, we had a total of seven boys and six girls, they each had their part to play in our lives, their own life-plans, paths of progression, and service to humanity.

The way our communities were set up meant the fact that I spent much time away from the family home undertaking my leadership duties did not have any impact on the children. Although we had family homes, the communities were arranged so that everyone looked out for everyone else, there was no concept of time or worry that children would "go missing" life flowed naturally in these community settings. There were volunteer childminders and women with whom the children would naturally gravitate, the children had much freedom and were allowed to develop unhindered, they did not have any formal education, but would spontaneously learn from their peers, they spent the majority of their time with their peers/friends, returning to the family home when they felt it necessary.

If a child developed a special interest in a given subject, they could request to be given a sort of apprenticeship, where a mentor would be designated. For example our third born child Amela showed an interest in spirituality and leadership, I recognised her as a soul from Rycia, she already had soul-knowledge and wisdom in her heart, so she joined me for an apprenticeship, and at the time of my death assumed the leadership role where I left off.

Our first born, Benfinator was a very sensitive soul with the gift of healing, combined with the ability to manipulate energy systems, he was a pioneer in these fields, and was able to teach the community how to direct and utilise these energies for the greater good. It was interesting to observe how Benfinator coped with the physicality of the Earth plane, I smiled when I observed him struggle with practical tasks, because I had faced similar sorts of challenges I was able to understand his frustration, after all, in our homelands we were able to simply think of something, and it would simply manifest, yet for us on Earth it was infinitely frustrating when we clearly set our intention to create and nothing happened!

Our second child, Edev, another boy, was full of kindness and concern for others, he was naturally empathic and was a care-giver from his heart, prior to his birth he experienced some doubts as to whether or not he wished to incarnate, this translated to me feeling a marked reduction in his foetal movements. Naturally I felt alarmed and concerned, so I tuned into his consciousness, I was able to reassure Edev that he would be loved and cared for very well, and asked him to revisit his life plan, what was that telling him he needed to do?

Our ninth born, Joxy, being of his father's elk was a gifted craftsman, he held regular masterclasses where he taught communities how to fashion products out of raw materials. Our youngest child, a girl named Simona had a natural affinity with nature and animals, the children in the community would look to her to teach them about the natural world, this included knowledge of crystals and jewels. All our children including those not mentioned here were unique, and held their special place. Due to the children being of such mixed heritage, this gave rise to any number of variables with regard to talents and gifts; it was very satisfying to observe that as family we were bringing a diverse range of knowledge into the communities.

With the help of our off-spring we set up a model for community existence that was in complete harmony with the spirit of the Earth. We modelled a life- style that showed how beneficial it was for individuals to regularly tune into their higher selves and relate to their spirit guides, this was incorporated into daily meditations, and felt natural.

Our communities were also very much in tune with the elemental dimensions, we were operating as one, every life form was honoured and respected. If we used plants, trees or rocks for building materials we would consult with the spirit of these beings, ask them for permission before utilising these resources. Similarly if we utilised plants for food or making healing potions, again we would then offer thanks to their spirits for offering themselves in service to us. We knew that we did not "own" these resources, we knew that the Earth was carefully balanced, even on an individual level we felt a sense of responsibility to ensure this balance was maintained.

We also taught the communities a fundamental understanding of energy systems and the potential impact of the collective consciousness on vibrational frequencies. We all felt a responsibility for maintaining the vibrational levels of planet Earth, should for any reason a fraction in this occur, then those in the community with the knowledge and skills to repair the systems were called upon.

Depending on the need of the individual situation, those repairing the energy system might take the form of dragon, unicorn or simply someone from the local community. Everyone accepted this as normal and natural, we all felt a deep connection to the spirit of the Earth, this gave us all a great sense of belonging, and despite the vast differences and diversity of our outward physical forms, we knew that of our true essence, we were all derived from the same Source. Although this was an immensely challenging lifetime, it was very satisfying to know we had left a legacy for the human race, in terms of skills and knowledge passed down through our children and their off-spring.

CHAPTER 4 – MORE TO COME

Now I will tell you about an existence where I served a warrior-type of function. A time when planet Earth was in a reasonably early phase of existence, at this time there were a lot of inquisitive visitors from other planets that held a certain curiosity about this new planet. Many visited simply to look around, a bit like when a new park or shopping centre opened, it might attract many curious visitors, it was the same for planet Earth at this time. As with the visitors to Rycia, most of the inter-galactic visitors were friendly and simply curious, wishing to visit, take a look round, then leave the Earth in peace to evolve via natural laws.

Occasionally visitors would arrive that were on recognisance missions, looking to see how other planets could be exploited for their own ends, unlike Rycia, Earth had not yet learned that a collective energy of universal love was the only effective way of keeping these unwanted guests at bay, therefore I was assigned to the task of gate-keeper or door-man.

Planet Earth had a number of portholes through which the inter-galactic visitors would gain access to the planet, at these portholes the energy was such that it allowed them to enter the Earth from these points, therefore my role was to be the over-seer of the portholes, and intervene if necessary. (Interestingly it can be observed that throughout the world today there are a number of religious buildings built on the sites of some of the portholes, although the true significance of these sites has been lost to the majority of people, it is curious to observe that on some levels peoples sub-conscious was in tune enough to deem the sites "sacred" and build some significant religious structures on these sites). For these incarnations I took on a griffin-like appearance, I had an eagle-like head, with a large lion-type body, I had huge wings, massive lion paws with sharp talons, a long tail with a triangle shaped end. I was granted much power for these life-times, I was literally fearless but in a compassionate and wise way. The way I took care of the portholes was mainly energetically, if I was alerted to a hostile influence approaching, I would summon up all my personal power, and would also ask my comrades from Rycia to remotely send their energy to raise the vibrational level of the portholes, this way it would make it extremely difficult for the majority of the hostile forces to enter Earth, as they simply could not transcend the high frequency energy of the portholes.

However, there was a race of visitors who had devoted significant time and resource in developing technology that was able to deceive and transmute a "fake" energy code, in this way they literally were able to go "under the radar" and slip though the Earthly portholes. They were a race of beings that were desperately trying to increase the vibrational level of their own planet, although they were wise enough to realise that increasing the collective energy of their people would benefit their planet, they were mistaken in the way they were going about this.

As a result they had collected up all the beings who's energy vibration was lower than what they deemed the desired levels, and were intending to banish these people to another planet – in this case planet Earth, in the hope that by removing this energy it would increase the collective energy of their own planet. This was not in the plan for planet Earth, they had slipped through the Earth porthole, and I was faced with trying to negotiate an amicable solution.

The visitors were adamant they were going to leave their "unwanted people" on planet Earth, and argued that by doing this, their own planet would become enlightened sooner. Further purporting that since planet Earth was relatively new; the people they left behind would integrate quickly, arguing that planet Earth had not yet evolved enough for their energy to be a problem to the planet.

My response was to point out to them that first and foremost by entering planet Earth under false pretences they had broken a Universal Law, and asked them if they thought doing that would help their cause for increased enlightenment? I also advised that they were misinformed if they thought that banishing a fraction of their people would ultimately increase the vibrational pattern of their own planet. As this too, was contra to Universal Law, which denoted that all life forms and beings were valuable and deserved to be integrated into the communities. The real value of spiritual development (and the secondary gain of increasing vibrational level) was determined on how well communities learned to adapt to each other and live in peace and harmony. They were not prepared to listen to me, and chose to deny and ignore the Universal Laws, as though in some way they thought they were exempt from them.

I felt a profound sinking feeling in my heart, for a brief moment I saw movie-type images of potential future scenes on planet Earth, this concerned me deeply, but then I reminded myself they were only potentials, all was not lost, if they were determined to leave these people here, the focus would need to be on "damage limitation". I also reminded myself that with some loving guidance and mentoring these people may learn spiritual truths and evolve naturally, though realistically I knew this would be a tough task as they were not "meant" to be here, Universal Laws had been contravened.

I wondered how this would impact on the evolution of planet Earth. This troubled me immensely, I felt I had failed in my task to protect the human race, I felt inadequate and disturbed, I knew that in order to restore my equilibrium I needed to consult with my guides and higher-self. I tuned in to this frequency, we held an emergency conference with the masters, indeed this was not in the plan, but now that it had happened, we were looking for a solution for the best way forward. In terms of my own sense of failing, I was reminded that I did not work in isolation, and that although I was subscribed a task, how could I be responsible for the others free will? I had done everything in my power to avert the situation, I could do no more; ruminating over this would serve me no valuable purpose, I calibrated this information, and placed my focus on to how we could best accommodate our uninvited and unexpected guests.

It was agreed that communities of the visitors would be integrated alongside the more established communities of humans, although their own people had treated them as such, they would certainly not be treated as prisoners or detainees, they would have freedom to move around unhindered. It was agreed that a mentorship programme be established, where volunteers would model appropriate Earth-dwelling behaviour, as it has to be remembered that these beings were from a different planet, so they had much to learn about their new environment and adapting to Earthly conditions. The native Earth-dwellers at these times had very trusting and open natures, so there were plenty of volunteer mentors, eagerly waiting to work with these new beings, the majority of humans felt compassion for this banished race, and genuinely wanted to help.

So it was with great vigour and enthusiasm that these visitors entered into the communities and mentorship programmes, however it soon became clear that there were some problems with the programmes. A high proportion of the visitors were not interested in learning about Earth ways, there were instances where the visitors manipulated and took control of their mentors, and actually began to give orders to their teachers - roles reversed. The native Earth dwellers found this extremely confusing, they had not encountered deception or blatant manipulation before, so they had no idea how to respond to it. Up until then, anyone in a position of power or authority would have held a degree of spiritual wisdom, having earned their position of respect. But now it seemed that the visitors had stepped into these roles, were issuing commands without the corresponding spiritual wisdom, resulting in decisions being made that were contra to the natural laws of the planet, and confusing for the original human race.

Due to the trusting and accommodating nature of the original humans, the visitors found it very easy to manipulate the people, and use them for their own ends. They were able to do this by persuading the original humans that their existing value system and way of life was out-dated and a bit silly, they put convincing arguments forward as to why it was better to adopt their own values (which were to the most part more self-centred, far less integrated and showed much less cooperation with others). The original humans had a natural instinct to accept advice from their leaders, and since the visitors had assumed leadership roles and asserted themselves into positions of power and control, it was not long before fractions of the community were adopting the life-styles more akin to the visitor's ways. The original humans were persuaded, cajoled and convinced that this was the most appropriate way to live their lives. They readily accepted the assertions of power and control the visitors imposed, which began to have an adverse effect on the spiritual and ethical values of the communities.

Naturally over time, the new visitors bred with the original humans, and a hybrid race of humans was created, eventually the pure visitor race became all but extinct. The visitor hybrids continued to manipulate resources, both from the natural world, and the resources of human toil and labour, to serve a select few. As a result, there was disruption to the natural balance, integration and appreciation of others in the collective, and in suffice to say that the energy vibration of the planet took a significant down turn of frequency, matter particles became much denser, to accommodate the energy patterns of the hybrids.

As such, there was much more of a distinction between matter and the etheric realms, the elemental species retreated to their etheric frequencies, they felt much safer there, as the majority of the hybrid humans were unable to see them. The elemental races had suffered extensively under the jurisdiction of the hybrid humans, as there had been numerous examples of where the elemental's opinions and wisdom had been overlooked and ignored, resulting in unwise choices being made with regard to the collection and distribution of Earth resources, as well as the locations of buildings and communities.

The Earth vibrational frequency had slowed down and lowered to accommodate the vibrational levels of the hybrid humans, but the elemental communities were still operating on a finer and faster vibration, as such, there was a natural separation of the two, instead of living in an integrated community, these were now two separate groups, journeying in different directions. Thus marked the beginning of humans' gradual migration away from the integration of their higher selves, and connection to the Earth Spirit in daily consciousness, and a shift towards them focussing more on their "here and now" life, with an emphasis on enhancing their material position, sometimes at the cost of other people, the environment, or the good of the community. This move corresponded more towards the current paradigm of life on Earth, rather than the original "enchanted" version.

For my own soul journey, this marked a difficult phase for me, I was struggling to separate my sphere of responsibility from the whole, and woefully mourned the loss of the enchanted Earth. I felt genuinely bereft that a high proportion of the human race had lost contact with the higher side of life, and were mistakenly pursuing paths that I could see would lead to much personal suffering. It was difficult enough to envisage personal suffering, but I could also see that disregarding the higher side of life, and losing the connection with the spirit of mother Earth could result in potential catastrophic disruption on a global scale. I repeatedly consulted with the elders, the message I was given was always the same, that I could not change past events, but could influence circumstances going forward.

This I resolved to do, I was determined that planet Earth would be loved, cherished and nurtured by all her inhabitants, as I knew this was vital for the well-being of all life-forms, as well as the planet herself. I was also determined that individuals would have a natural insight to their spirituality and life-purpose, as again I knew this was essential for the well-being of individuals as well as the collective consciousness, which in turn effected the whole of the planet. I wanted to ensure that the inhabitants of planet Earth maintained their true integrity as beings, therefore I pledged to undertake as many incarnations as was necessary to undertake this task, and chose them to correspond with where I felt I would be of most influence.

I will now give some brief examples of some of the lives I have lead, it has to be remembered that I have had countless incarnations, the ones mentioned here are just a very small sample: Moving towards the most recent phase in Earth's existence, during one life as a male I was subscribed the task of over- seeing the building of tombs. Before incarnation the plan was for me to use my knowledge of sound manipulation in order to manipulate matter, and manifest the buildings. This method had been the usual way of construction in earlier phases of Earth inhabitation, and had by no means been seen as unconventional. However, the situation I was put in was not as planned, the leaders in this instance were mainly human hybrids. Because they themselves had no knowledge of sound manipulation, and were unable to access the frequency necessary for it to work they had disregarded the sound method as invalid. They held me captive, and literally prevented me from using my knowledge. They had contaminated the energy fields, and had made it impossible for me to use this method of construction. Instead they had rounded up hundreds of native people (mainly original humans) against their will, enslaved them, and had insisted that they physically build the tombs manually.

I was distraught when I realised what was going on, I pleaded and pleaded for them to let the people go, and explained that given the correct energetic conditions manual labour would not be necessary. Unfortunately the leaders would not accept what I was saying. It was as though they were so invested in their own position of being "right" they were not willing to let me manifest the tombs by sound. This would have saved much human suffering and time, but it wasn't to be. It was as though the leaders enjoyed holding power over the workers, as though they benefitted in some way from seeing them toil and suffer, it seemed as though they were obsessed with the position of superiority they held over the enslaved workers. Once the physical construction was under-way, they released me from captivity, and insisted I "oversaw" the project. To me this was a complete farce. How could I manage a project that had caused so much needless suffering for humanity? I used my position to try to improve circumstances for the enslaved people, and attempted to negotiate better conditions, but despite my tenacious efforts, any gains made were marginal. I was however able to offer a small amount of comfort to these people, I would visit their living accommodation, provide counsel and tell them stories about the enchanted Earth. These stories were passed down through the ages, and form some of the "myths" and "legends" we know today. My life review of this incarnation saw me sad that again I felt I had not achieved what I had intended, but as always it would seem I had done everything I could within my powers, the rest was down to others' free will.

Moving yet closer towards the present day, I had a happy incarnation as a male beggar living in India, hundreds of years ago, I lived by the road-side and spent much of my time singing. This was a joyful time, my lack of social status and material possessions had encouraged me to tune into the spiritual frequencies. I felt wholly complete in this life, my purpose was to model to others that it was possible to be joyful, even when living on the brink of survival existence.

I undertook many simple and unremarkable lives, such as a European farmer's daughter in the middle ages, where my main job was to sell onions and produce from the farm. I also lived in Eastern Europe in the 18th century as a spinster, the 12th century saw me as a female prostitute/courtesan. I lived as a peasant boy in ancient Tibet, a Sadhu healer in India, and a community leader in Celtic Britain. Some of these lives were more successful (spiritually) than others; one has to remember that I was incarnated as a regular human being, and was subject to all the potential weaknesses being human entailed. I had incarnations where I all but lost touch with my spiritual self, made mistakes in relationships, let greed and ego get the better of me, was selfish and unkind. Then karma would assert itself and I would spend many more life-times putting right the wrongs I had done, paying off the karmic debts, these lives tended to be more mundane and about "me" than the more purposeful spiritual incarnations. Looking back I would say that the ratio of male/female incarnations were roughly the same, though often during times where patriarchal societies dominated, if it was an incarnation where my life plan was to be of influence I took incarnations as males.

Other incarnations saw me living as Native Americans both before and after the invasion of the white people. During these lifetimes there was an essence of purity within most of these communities. I was able to live my lives fully integrated with nature and the Great Spirit, it was almost like the earlier times on Earth, where the spirits of trees, rivers and animals were recognised and revered within our culture, a beautiful and fulfilling way to live a human life-time. Our tribe was particularly attuned to nature and other realms. Our community life was completely reliant on communication with the spirit of the Earth. Within our community everyone without exception communicated on some psychic level with the ancestors, these would be relatives of the tribe living in the spirit world, or animals or tree spirits that had a connection with the community. Everyone felt a strong connection to nature and other realms; this was simply "normal" and made up the very fabric of our daily lives. We would receive guidance from the spirit of the Earth as to where and when to sow crops, we would also use knowledge of energy systems to feed and nourish the plants. It was reciprocal; we honoured and respected nature and the Earth spirit, and in turn it would look after us. A wonderful example of how it is possible for humans to live in complete harmony with all living things.

In order to survive the harsh winter conditions, it was necessary for us to hunt the bison on the Great Plains, without their sustenance there was no doubt we would not have survived. Our hunts took on a spiritual meaning, and hunting was in fact a very humbling experience for all involved. Prior to the hunt we would engage in a community ceremony where we would communicate with the collective spirit energy of the bison, we would ask if any of the animals would be prepared to sacrifice their lives, in order to facilitate our survival as a species.

The bison gave to us generously, and we truly appreciated their service, we knew it was an integral part of our own survival and we were grateful to these magnificent creatures. We would endeavour to kill the animals in the most pain-free way possible, and at all times we held love, respect and gratitude to the spirit of the bison for their generosity to us. Following the hunt we would hold another community ceremony to give thanks and honour the spirits of the bison we had hunted, we would also ask that their spirits would be safely guided to the spirit world, where they would meet with the collective of other bison.

It might be hard to believe, but the hunt was a cooperative experience, we would communicate telepathically with the animals, and would know where and when to find them. We would also be guided towards the individual animals that had offered themselves to us, it was a carefully managed, humbling and respectful experience. Completely different to the random adrenaline-fuelled hunts, one might observe, were there is no respect held for the life forces being killed, where animals are seen as a commodity, resource, or trophy, where their essence and spirit is totally overlooked and disregarded. Another feature of our community life at that time was the shamans and medicine men and women, their roles would be spiritual leaders and healers. They would have the gift of communication with other realms and would regularly consult with these other realms at times of difficulties, often bringing in higher knowledge to help solve problems. They also held the knowledge of plants and herbs, and knew how to create potions and drafts that would serve the purpose of healing. Some of the potions were also used by the shamans to help them journey to other realms, or they might be used to heal the landscape or rivers, should that be necessary.

When preparing the potions one of the most important aspects of the preparation was for the shaman to link directly with the spirit of the plant/herbs being used. After asking for permission, they would invite the spirit of the plants to imbue their wisdom and essence-energy into the potion. Again this was done with the upmost respect, and thanks were given to the plants, and the collective energy of that particular plant species. It was observed that should the spirit of the plant not be considered and consulted, then it was highly unlikely that the potion would be effective or be of any use or help. Our communities understood that all life-forms were linked, and all life-forms deserved to be respected and honoured. We did not think we owned the land, or that it was there simply to serve our purpose, we knew we were part of a large cycle of life, and our life-styles reflected this understanding.

A scattering of Native Americans at that time were not as peaceful as our tribe, although they held the knowledge of the Earth spirit, they tended to use it for darker purposes, were war-hungry and thrived on conflict. When the invasion of the white people came, the propaganda put forward by the invading white people tended to be stories from the less peaceful minority fraction of the Native American population; therefore the popular stories concerning Native Americans tend to be about blood-thirsty "Indians" that liked nothing more than scalping enemies. That account was inaccurate, as the majority of the Native American people were peace-loving gentle souls that revered nature and the interconnectedness of life.

I wondered if by portraying the Native Americans as war-hungry and barbaric, that in some way that gave the invaders some justification for their own violent actions; generate an idea of a threatening enemy, then on some levels their own actions seemed more relevant and justifiable. I pondered this, and wondered how many other wars throughout human history had been subject to similar inaccurate propaganda?

My final life as a Native American saw me as an Indian Chief during the time of the invasion of the white people; once again I was tasked with negotiating a satisfactory peace plan. As history indicates, this proved to be impossible, the white people taking complete control and dominance, and marginalising the Natives to designated reservations. One of the hardest things for me to comprehend during this life-time was to observe the white people, and see how spiritually dead their lives really were. They appeared to talk of a "God the Father" yet talking about "him" was all they appeared to do.

There didn't seem to be any interaction with the Great Spirit, I could find no evidence of them connecting to their higher selves or wisdom from other realms. They seemed to think that animals, plants and the land itself was there simply for their use and purpose. A resource to be plundered, used then simply disregarded, without taking any regard for the inner essence or spirit of the animal, plant or mineral.

This philosophy was hugely confusing for us, as it was at such variance to what we knew in our hearts was the truth. We could see that the majority of the white people had no quality of soul happiness; they appeared to be driven by a deep seated sense of dissatisfaction, as though they were compelled to accumulate as many material possessions as possible, with a sad disregard for the value and essence of that which they declared ownership over.

I was able to quickly learn their language and conversed with them with ease, what I found much, much more difficult to understand was their spiritually void outlook on life, and what appeared to be their insatiable desire to dominate, conquer and claim. It was interesting to observe that they believed us to be "savages" that needed taming, yet from our point of view there was so much we could teach them about the reality of life, their own personal soul journeys, mother Earth, the universe and the part we all play in this as human beings.

We could have also taught them how to be happy and contented from a soul perspective, because from what we observed their life-styles were taking them further and further away from this. We so much wanted to share this with them, but unfortunately, they simply ridiculed us, their minds completely closed to any attempts by us to offer any wisdom.

Despite this, I persisted with my attempts to negotiate a satisfactory way of integrating the white community with ours. However they were not prepared to meet us half way, they felt that our way of life was fundamentally wrong, believing their ways were superior, and that our way of life should be either eradicated or failing that, marginalised and moved out of the way.

As I watched the desecration of our communities, my heart sank. I observed the vital force and the energy frequency of our world decline and become heavier and denser. I also observed the confusion and utter despair of our people; they knew that this new way introduced by the white invaders could only lead to personal unhappiness for all humans for generations to come, and we were worried that communities were being formed that had no awareness of the importance of honouring the Great Spirit and all life forms with whom we share the planet. We were most concerned about the impact this philosophy would have on the spiritual well-being of the planet, mother Earth herself, as well as the human race.

For me on a soul level this situation triggered memories of my former failed negotiations with the "uninvited visitors". Just like before, my negotiations proved futile, and again I had a vision of a movie-type image of potential life on the continent, where nature and spiritual life could be disregarded in the pursuit of personal material gain. I saw horrific wars motivated by personal power and ego, and exploitation of the masses, to serve a "select" and privileged group of individuals, where the only chance one had of becoming a world leader was to be able to buy oneself into the position of electable candidate. So different from the earlier times where community leaders were chosen for their wisdom and compassion.

As I watched the movie image of potentials, I observed chaos and disruption to the Earth's energy systems resulting in unpredictable and erratic weather systems and an increase in "natural disasters". Native Americans believed that weather was a primary indicator as to the health and well-being of our planet Earth. Any devastating weather systems would be a direct reflection of how our mother Earth was bearing up. I wondered how our beautiful Earth would survive if the masses disregarded her being, and did not look after her and nourish her as we had. I could only hope that these potentials would not materialise, and that humans would turn around their way of thinking, before they destroyed themselves and the planet.

As I reviewed this image of the potential future of planet Earth, my body trembled and I was overcome with a profound sense of dread, but I was powerless to do anymore. I asked myself how it could be, that so many of the human race could potentially lose their connection to their true inner-essence and spiritual purpose. From what I could see many would be misled into mistakenly pursuing paths of material gratification, with a total disregard for their spirit and soul, and an incomprehensible indifference for the well-being of planet Earth.

Just then the image I was watching changed, it became brighter and lighter somehow, this was a very different picture indeed, I could see a potential for a community that felt cooperative and valued everyone equally, a place where there was a value system in place that championed care for others and respect for nature and all beings. My heart skipped a beat as I focussed in. I wanted to see more; I was seeing a community setting that looked the size of a large village; with beautiful buildings that looked as though they had been crafted from natural stone and marble, with exquisite window art.

There was a stream running through the centre of the civilisation that seemed to be singing as it meandered through the village, the water emitted an iridescent glow, the surrounding Earth and landscape looked alive and vibrant, the energy felt positive and uplifting. I looked upon what I assumed were domestic residences, these looked tidy and well looked after; it felt as though there was lots of open space with trees and vegetation in abundance. I was wondering where all the people were, but then I found myself observing what seemed to be like some sort of community event, where everyone was sitting together amongst a circle of huge trees, eyes almost closed, chanting some undeterminable phrases. There was such an atmosphere of calm and joy, I wondered what it was they were doing?

All of a sudden I found myself linking up with the collective consciousness of the group, it would seem that they were taking part in a sort of group meditation, where they were giving thanks for all that had been provided for them from the universe and at the same time honouring mother Earth, whilst sending her energy and love.

I could also see that as a collective they were asking for guidance and wisdom in order to live their lives in harmony with the other beings with which they shared the planet. It felt like this was a two-way communication, and that people were actually tuning into their higher-selves and receiving guidance from the Great Spirit. I felt a rush of hope and optimism to think that this really could be a potential for our beloved planet Earth, this kind of life really was a possibility, if it were to become a reality, then my work as a Rycian would be nearer to completion, and the human race and planet Earth would be a step closer to enlightenment and ultimate freedom.

As the images faded I couldn't help but wonder which of these potentials was most likely to play out. As I considered the current circumstances of the invasion of the white people, the desecration of our community life-style and all things truly spiritual, the first scenario seemed the most likely outcome. However, the second scene was also a real potential, it would just depend on which way the collective consciousness of the human race decided to go. When I took my transition from this life back into the spirit world, again my life review saw me immensely sad for all the spiritual knowledge that had been disregarded. I had to accept that the world was entering a dark phase, but I was reminded not to lose hope, the second scenario was still a possibility. I considered the numerous phases the Earth had undertaken through eons of Earthly time, and I knew that I had to trust that just like the phoenix and the fire, regeneration would take place and eventually things would come good.

However, much as I tried, I could not quell the uneasiness arising in my being when considering exactly how difficult things would get before the regeneration would take place. On a soul level it felt very much like deja vous, I had faced this situation in different phases of Earth's development many times before, and I wondered just how much mother Earth could cope with, and exactly how many chances was she willing to give us?

CHAPTER 5 – FINDING SELF

My final Native American incarnation marked a phase in human development which corresponded with a further downturn in human consciousness in terms of its connectedness with nature and the spirit world. History leads us to believe that following on from that era the industrial revolution took place, or maybe as we are now discovering, the last "reset" occurred. This forced people into working even harder to survive, which in turn gave even more potential for humanity to disconnect from their spiritual values.

During these times I was still trying to undertake incarnations where I could be of benefit and help to humanity. For one particular life in the early 1800's I chose to incarnate as a rich English gentleman. I had been brought up in luxury; every material wish had been satisfied, with servants attending to my every need, living in a large country estate my father being the "Lord of the Manor." Growing up I had lead a sheltered life, and had been lead to believe that the wealth that surrounded me was due to inheritance, and was told about the merits of that system of life, where the people on the estate enjoyed working for my father, and indeed took pride in their roles. Perhaps due to my naivety, from what I could observe, this did seem to be the case, my father appeared to be a kind and fair master, I never witnessed any abuse of power and the estate workers seemed happy and contented with their lot.

I lived in blissful ignorance until I reached my early 20's when it was decided I would accompany my uncle on a business trip. I was excited and exhilarated to take the over-seas voyage to the West Indies. I had a natural inclination towards travel, yet up until then, the farthest I had journeyed was to France. Steam trains were in their infancy, with a few rudimentary lines existing here and there, but as yet the national networks had yet to have been established, so travelling distance was not such a common occurrence.

During the long sea journey to the West Indies, I was dreadfully seasick, but tried hard to put on a brave face. I did not want to appear weak or inferior to neither my uncle nor my male cousin with whom I was travelling. I was looking forward to being initiated into the family business, and fulfil my duties.

However, my boyhood fantasies and illusions were soon to be shattered, as the cruel reality of the situation unfolded. I could hardly believe what I saw as we visited our family's sugar plantations. For the first time in my life I was faced with human degradation and poverty on a scale as yet unimaginable to me. I witnessed the stench of unkempt, emaciated bodies, a sea of haunted, expressionless eyes, their spirits all but extinguished. These people were barley given enough food and water to survive; their entire life consisted of working in the plantations, no time off, no freedom, no basic human rights.

What was equally disturbing was the matter-of-fact acceptance of this by my family. I could feel my inner-being calling to me that this was not right, my soul churned with discord, and before long it dawned on me that these poor creatures were in fact enslaved people! I had been told stories that the workers in the West Indies had similar lives to our estate workers, it had not occurred to me that they were captured people. I felt sick to my stomach, I found it overwhelming and difficult to comprehend, I felt racked with guilt, to think that the lavish and extravagant life-style I had indulged in, and the luxuriant wealth enjoyed by our family and peers in England was in fact a product of greedy exploitation of fellow human beings. I wanted to scream and shout that this was not fair, how could our family be a part of all this?

When I questioned my uncle about the living conditions of the people, I was told that until recently they had been bound in chains, and that they were technically "free" to leave, but they had all chosen to stay from their own free will, because they liked living there. As he spoke it was as though he honestly believed we were offering these people benevolence! I listened politely, but I could feel the restlessness and anger arising in my blood, what other choice had these people got? They had been captured and enslaved, estranged from their families, and forced to work as slaves. They had zero personal power, even if they had wanted to attempt to return to their homelands, there was no transport, and they had no means of trading as they had no independent possessions or money. How was that benevolent?

It infuriated me that I was being told that they enjoyed working there and had chosen to stay, when in fact they were trapped. The reality of their situation was reflected in their eyes, almost everyone had haunted eyes, they looked so tremendously sad and empty, like their life-energy and dignity had been stripped away. Until that trip, I had not seen anyone of African origin before. I was fascinated by the beautiful colour of the peoples' skin, their abundant black hair, and their muscular bodies, although many looked emaciated and malnourished, they still looked beautiful to me.

One day early on in my visit I was walking across the yard when a house maid bowed to me and said she was pleased to make my acquaintance. I was surprised by this unprecedented behaviour, but I had always struggled to treat servants as "inferior" and I had been in trouble countless times in my younger days for breaking with protocol. I found it very amusing that a young maid of around eleven years old had the confidence to speak to me in this manner. I noticed that she was nowhere near as dark skinned as the rest of the people here, in some ways her mannerisms held a familiarity. I thought I would reward her boldness, and asked her to show me the way to the plantation, as she had risked a lot to approach me in this way, and I wondered what it was she wanted to say to me.

She told me that her mother had been chosen by the "other master" (my father), to be what she called one of his "special friends". She told me that her mother had been very proud to be of assistance to the master, because it meant she was taken from the plantation and given house duties instead. The girl told me that after she was born, her mother had been allowed to stay in the servants' quarters of the house, that was until her premature death a few years later, after which the girl had assumed maid duties and had also been allowed to stay in the servants' quarters of the house.

It did not take me long to realise that in fact I was standing face to face with my half-sister! Our eyes locked. It seemed that she was desperate for me to acknowledge our blood tie, I had always wanted a sister, and here I had one, but I knew that she would never be acknowledged as anything more than a servant. On a soul level this felt so unfair and wrong, I wanted so much to reach out and embrace the sibling experience; the class and caste system felt so out of sync with what I knew in my heart was the way of the Great Spirit and natural law. I contemplated on what I could practically do to help pioneer some changes in this respect, and meanwhile made up some superficial excuse to necessitate my sister's maid services, so that I could get to know her a bit better.

The whole unpleasant truth about our family business in the West Indies, forced me to grow up rapidly. I found it all extremely difficult to comprehend and take in. I experienced a type of psychic shock, my world as I saw it would never be the same again, I could not accept or be a part of this terrible slave trade. The truth was I was so overcome by what I saw that I simply went dumb-struck, I could not find my voice, I went completely in on myself, lost a quarter of my body weight, and was totally unable to function.

The physician put my condition down to an unknown tropical disease, and decided the best course of action would be to send me home, yet I knew in my heart it was not a tropical disease, but a soul-shock reaction, my responses had literally frozen due to the trauma I had experienced witnessing the horrendous truth. There were no other words to describe the situation than sheer human exploitation. On a soul level this took me right back to the experiences of the unwanted visitors, who exploited the original humans. I felt ashamed that due to my ignorance, up until then I had colluded with this exploitation, and had been happy to live a life of luxury provided for by the slave trade. This drove my resolve to help banish ignorance; surely, if people were aware of the truth then they would not want to knowingly exploit others for their own ends would they?

The long voyage home enabled me a period of reflection and recuperation, I felt determined to share my findings with my mother and my older brother. Surely they too were unaware of the truth of the situation. I felt confident we could find a better way of life for the people and give them more humane living conditions and some independence, even if that meant a reduction in profit and productivity. Surely that would be a fairer solution and we would all be able to sleep better at night.

I had always been reasonably close to my mother, so with a degree of enthusiasm as to my proposed new business model I broached the subject with her. My mother's reaction was totally unexpected and truly shocking. She said the people working the plantations were nothing more than animals and savages that did not need anything more than what was provided for them. She said that by placing them on the plantations, we were in fact helping them move away from their uncouth life-styles, and she truly believed that we were doing them some sort of favour and service. She strongly advised me to forget my "fanciful" ideas, and in no uncertain terms warned me that if I pursued what she called my ridiculous notion, then it would have grave implications for myself, and my place in the family.

I wondered what she meant by that, but if she was referring to cutting me from any financial assistance, then I was prepared to be poor, my inner conscience would not allow me to knowingly live a life of ease at the expense of all those poor wretched people. I'd already experienced a great shock to my psyche having witnessed the plantations and slave-trade first hand, but to hear my mother speaking like that was beyond my comprehension, I could only speculate that she'd reached that opinion because she'd never visited the plantations first-hand so was unaware of the squalor and hardship of the people there. Also at those times women were purposely excluded from any kind of business knowledge or politics, they were only told half-truths, so I was prepared to excuse her ignorance.

Following my mother's unexpected reaction, I approached my older brother with a degree of caution and I tried to convince myself that he would see things from my point of view. After all he had not got the excuse of ignorance that my mother had, he himself had visited the plantations so surely had more awareness of the situation there. I outlined my new business model to my brother, and mentioned that I had already pledged my support to the implementation of the abolishment of the slave trade.

Hearing this my brother exploded with anger, he lifted me up by the scruff of my neck, raged and shook me violently. Venomously defending the family's dealings in the West Indies. I was taken aback by his reaction and calmly asked him to let me go, begged him to hear me out, and see that there was another way of doing things. He was not prepared to listen, he continued to wage a personal attack, accusing me of being weak sentimental and above all irresponsible. He felt I was compromising the family's livelihood for the sake of "a few insignificant savages".

To hear him refer to those beautiful people in those terms struck a chord in my inner being. At that precise moment, I became conscious of my task and reason for that incarnation. I knew in that instant that I would do everything I could in my power to help these people, and I knew I had to choose the people before my family. I felt a huge sense of sadness to lose my family in this way, but the family I thought I had were already lost to me anyway, they were strangers and not the warm-hearted loving beings I had held in such regard until then. I retired to my bed that evening emotionally worn to the core, I was experiencing a cocktail of emotions, guilt for the plantation workers, sadness at the loss of my family, frustration and anger that they refused out-right to hear my proposals and work towards a solution for everyone.

It was hard to walk away, but I had to listen to my soul and do what I knew in my heart was the right thing. I invested my energies with the anti-slavery movement. As you can imagine my family took this as a direct attack and insult on them, they withdrew any financial assistance, and banished me from the family. This did not concern me greatly, I earned an income as a clerk and letter writer, and did the odd bit of teaching here and there. I rented a small inexpensive room above an Inn, I still had my good quality clothing so my material needs were more than adequately met. In fact, it felt quite a relief that I was not living off the backs of the slaves anymore.

As time went on I was summoned to the family home for dinner. Entering the family estate after an extended period of absence felt almost surreal and alien, the luxuriant surroundings that I had once looked upon as beautiful and artful now looked ugly, crude and grotesque. Knowing where the money had come from to fund such luxury, I found it impossible to see things any other way. In my naivety, I thought this invitation may be a chance for reconciliation, and thought maybe their conscience had finally motivated them to do the right thing, and adopt my proposed model for the plantation workers. Again, I had completely misread my family's intentions; they had summoned me to demand that I stopped my anti-slavery work with immediate effect. Of course, I was unable to offer them any reassurance, and consequently the tensions between my family and I became more and more intense. I had a strong intuition that something was very wrong. I was unable to quell an intense sense of unease in the pit of my stomach. I had no appetite for the excessive dinner that was served at the family dining table, my mind drifted back to the plantation workers and the meagre rations of gruel they were afforded.

After dinner my brother and I withdrew to the drawing room, he poured himself a very large glass of cognac, and continued with the barrage of threats and ultimatums. When I did not agree to the family's demands, my brother became more and more enraged, he had been drinking heavily throughout dinner. The feeling in the pit of my stomach became ever more pronounced. Suddenly my brother stood up and threw the crystal cognac glass at me. I did not like what I saw in his eyes so began to make a hasty retreat. I dashed out of the French doors, and ran through the gardens to the estate boundary. The new train line had recently been laid nearby; I thought if I made it to there, it would be relatively easy to navigate the darkness on the train track. It was a damp autumn night, my "good shoes" did not offer much grip in the slippery conditions of the fallen autumn leaves. My brother had sent his dogs out, along with a local man he'd employed as a groundsman, although on this occasion it would appear he'd also employed him as a bounty hunter, and to my horror I realised that the bounty being hunted was in fact me!

Sheer primitive terror surged through my body, I ran as fast as I could, negotiating the railway sleepers, as hard as I tried I could not make my legs move any quicker. I had still not physically recovered from my trip to the West Indies, it felt like I was running in slow motion, I glanced ahead and saw the bridge. Alas the bridge, if I could make it there, I had a chance of survival, as I knew railway workers would be there and no-one would kill me in front of witnesses.

But the dogs reached me first, they were big powerful black hounds, it did not take much for them to bring me down, I felt a sharp searing pain in my right calf muscle as their jaws clamped around my leg. The powerful hounds held me down, I struggled to move and writhe on the train track. I could smell the fresh tar from the newly instated wooden railway sleepers, then I caught sight of the axe. I summoned all my power to move, but it was in vain, the axe repeatedly clobbered my head. I heard an enormous crack, followed by intense pain, the taste of blood, and felt warm blood gushing down my face, my teeth were missing. I was locked in a horrific scene of terror, confusion and desperation.

But then suddenly I felt a wonderful sense of peace and calmness wash over me, I knew in an instant that I was taking my transition back to the spirit world. I saw the light, then in complete consciousness observed myself leaving my poor battered body. It was over, no more pain. I was ok.

Although I had taken my transition, due to the acute shock and circumstance of my death, I hovered around the scene of my death for a few days before fully returning to the light of the spirit world, it felt important for me to do this. I observed the scene of chaos and charged emotions when the family and estate workers realised what had taken place. I had been murdered because I had refused to collude with slavery.

I saw the anguish and regret in my brother's face when he sobered up and realised the consequences of his actions. We had been very close, and had shared a genuine brotherly love, I was sure he had not meant to have had me killed, but it was too late. I was dead. Nothing could bring me back.

I wondered what karmic circumstances my brother would inherit in his subsequent lives, as he would need to pay off the karma he had created by his actions. Despite the fact he had instructed my murder, I felt a surge of love and compassion for him, I knew this was a soul connection, we had been together during countless lifetimes on Earth previously, I knew our paths would cross in future lives, and in a strange kind of way I looked forward to that. It. might be hard to understand, but I instantly forgave him.

During my life review I felt aggrieved that my early death meant I was prevented from implementing my plan to improve living conditions for our plantation workers. This sat heavily in my heart. I considered my last few incarnations, and acknowledged that I had experienced particularly high levels of trauma during these, there seemed to be a theme. I had tried so hard to bring about important changes for the well-being of humankind, but it felt to me I had not achieved very much at all.

However my guides reminded me that my good intentions had created a pathway of energy, that would be beneficial for humankind in future, because of my work the energetic pathways had been formed, so any subsequent work on these lines would be easier. I had to take heart from that, but I was still weary and my soul felt spent, so it was decided that I would take a period of respite and return to Rycia, for some healing and recuperation.

My guides and helpers accompanied me back to Rycia, I needed their support as the traumatic circumstances of my last death, coupled with the adversity experienced in my last few incarnations had depleted my energy system. It felt like utter bliss to be reunited with my homeland. I spent a period of time in the healing sanctuary, where my energy system was recharged, I had time to reflect on my Earthly experiences, and obtain further guidance as to my future aspirations. I also spent some precious time with my beloved soul family, it was so good to be home!

Having a period of reflection made me realise how challenging the Earthly conditions had become, especially in this latest phase of Earth life. From that removed perspective, it seemed obvious that the inhabitants of the planet were at a juncture where many were moving further towards materialism and further away from every day spiritual awareness. This paradigm appeared to be gathering momentum in the collective consciousness, it was no wonder that I had felt depleted and needed a period of respite, because that way of being was the opposite of all I had ever tried to perpetuate for planet Earth.

I knew that the only way humans would find peace and perfectly harmonious conditions (such as on Rycia) was through cultivating loving and cooperative communities, that honoured all living beings including that of the planet Earth herself, I was ready to return to Earth and continue my work.

From Earth-time perspective I had been absent for over a hundred years. During this time science had moved on, with significant developments in computer science, information technology, and the invention of the internet, there were now portable devices that enabled the world to communicate verbally and with video images instantly, from anywhere in the world, in a way that would be incomprehensible during my previous incarnation just over one hundred years before.

So it was into this world I took my next incarnation. In my life-plan I had chosen quite difficult circumstances for my childhood, this was to ensure that I remained true to myself, and would remain open to my spirituality and life beyond the obvious. Experiencing adversity carried the potential for character building and developing resilience. However in order for conditions to be favourable for the former, one had to remain in the window of tolerance, having life too easy and straight forward was unlikely to bring about development of character and resilience. On the other hand, conditions that were too tough would not bring about this either, as at those times we were more likely just to switch to survival mode. Of course it was all very well having a life plan, but the conditions one finds oneself in are more often than not influenced by the free will and actions of others. There were times when the free will of others had perhaps gone astray and their chosen behaviours were almost too challenging, too domineering, and I was at risk of shutting down completely.

Somehow, the more this happened, the more I found my inner-world. I was very aware of the different realms of existence, and was able to link with my spirit guide/guardian angel quite easily. During these times, the majority of the population of my culture were completely ignorant of any spiritual existence, so if I ever mentioned my reality to anyone else, I would be shut down and classed as weird.

From an early age I began to rely on myself, and realised that it really did not matter what opinion anyone else had of me, as long as I knew in my heart I was doing the right thing. I found it difficult not to speak the truth, and due to this I was seen as quite out-spoken. I did not fear authority; I struggled to esteem people simply because they held a title or position of power. I tended to naturally esteem people for their kindness and wisdom rather than their social status.

Justice was important to me, for example when I was a young girl of around nine, I had a teacher at school who I observed to be a bully, he picked on certain pupils and one day he was mocking a child that had special needs. I stood up and confronted him, and asked him why he felt the need to humiliate the other child. I was promptly marched to the head mistress' office, was not allowed to explain the reasons for my challenge, and was given lines as punishment. This did not bother me in the slightest, as in my heart I knew I had done the right thing in challenging him, though to some I might have been seen as naughty or misbehaving.

On another occasion, I recall being asked to draw dinosaurs; I drew mine brightly coloured with pink and yellow spots. The teacher told me off and said I'd been silly for drawing them that colour. I recall replying that no one knew what colour the dinosaurs were, as we were only assuming they were brownish, but nobody knew for sure! Again I was classed as being "naughty" but to me I was only stating what I felt was right. Despite situations like these, I loved school, I loved to learn and I always had plenty of friends.

On a few occasions during school assembly I might find myself having spontaneously left my body, floating above the assembly hall. I found it exhilarating and exciting watching myself and my friends from above. I might move my consciousness to the stage area and have a good look round, before daring myself to leave it to the last minute possible before re-entering my body. I was aware that at these times this would have been classed as very unusual behaviour and if I would have told anyone about my experiences they would have sent me for a mental health assessment, more than likely been diagnosed with a serious mental health condition, and heavily medicated.

I learned to keep my spiritual dalliances to myself, because I knew that everyone around me would find them completely unacceptable. However, a greater part of me knew that I'd undertaken these practices many times before, hundreds and thousands of years ago in different times and cultures when astral travel would have been seen as a normal daily practice.

In this way, I often felt alone, as no one I knew experienced life as I did, but in a spiritual sense, I always felt companionship and knew I was loved very much.

As well as my spontaneous daytime jaunts, I would often go astral travelling during sleep state. I would meet with my guides and we would journey to other realms, or sometimes just around the world. I loved these travels and looked forward to them. As that life progressed, I stepped even more into everyday spiritual awareness, to the point where when I met key people such as relatives or partners; often I would be able to naturally discern my soul connection with them, and see the reasons we had been incarnated together in this life.

For example, the brother that had me killed in my previous life entered this life as a boyfriend. I sensed he loved and cared for me very much, interestingly he had a strong aversion to alcohol. Whilst in the relationship with him I spontaneously regressed the past life we had shared, and could see the part he had played with regard to my previous death. I could see that his aversion to alcohol in this life, was due to him being blind drunk when he sanctioned my previous death, and that he had carried the deep regret and remorse into this life-time.

In touch with my higher-self, I was aware that the relationship was not meant to be in this lifetime, it was not in our life-plans. However, it was in his life-plan to experience losing me when he wanted the relationship to continue. From a karmic point of view he needed to experience the pain and anguish of this, as he had caused others to feel this way, when he had been responsible for the curtailment of my previous life. We parted amicably and with much love and affection made a pact to see each other in the next life. When observed from this view-point, I realised the impermanence of situations, understood that the present life was such a fraction, just a single facet of the complex diamond of who and what we really were.

I observed that often people denied the notion of impermanence and clung fiercely to the idea of life as they knew it. For example, any discussion around death and dying was seen as, at best in bad taste, at worst totally taboo and off- limits, and yet death was the only thing we could be certain of in life. It was as though if people did not mention death, then somehow that would be a protective factor against it. Then when for example a very elderly relative died, they would be hit with total shock and dis-belief, or they might feel anger towards the health care profession for not being able to keep their ninety- year-old relative alive. Perhaps having lost sight of the fact that there was a wisdom operating at a level much higher than even the most proficient doctor. I noticed that the pain and suffering of bereavement seemed to be significantly intensified when viewed form the point of view that they had lost their loved one forever. I wanted to reach out to these people and tell them they were mistaken, that their loved ones were doing all right in the afterlife, and chances were they would meet again, and even have subsequent lives together. I wanted to tell people to view their bereavement as though it was just a temporary separation, and to just think of it as though they had moved to another country far away. That one day they would be together again, but when one thinks of their current life as the sum total of everything they are or ever will be, it was very difficult to convey that message.

Looking back on this life-time, it is fair to say that out of all my countless previous incarnations on Earth, it was this life-time that I felt most like an alien. Life on Earth at these times seemed so at variance from life on Rycia. I really did feel a trillion miles away from home. My natural spiritual inclinations were little understood by the populations, not only that, they were truly seen as pathological.

Yet at the same time I observed that the majority of the human race were devoid of any true awareness of their own spirit or that of nature and mother Earth. I pondered this and wondered how it had come to be, that so many people were so disconnected from the natural rhythms and cycles of life, their higher-selves, their inner-wisdom, so therefore suffered so much as a consequence.

Most people in the developed world were using internet communication, there were social media forums, where people from all over the world could link together on-line, this enabled people from diverse cultural background and communities to link together and share ideas and philosophies. Prior to the development of internet communication, these philosophies and ideas would have been operating in isolation, so internet communication had opened up an entirely new forum for sharing ideas and perspectives.

During these times, most people marvelled at the "technology" that had become available, they were proud of the microchip and nanotechnology. Of course what the human psyche had forgotten, was that in earlier cycles of Earth existence, physical manifestation of such "technology" had not been necessary, as people were able to communicate telepathically. In times gone by, instead of sending a text, electronic message or phone call, they would have simply tuned in psychically, and telepathically exchanged their messages. But as the vibrational frequency of the planet had decreased this was no longer possible for most people, so humans began to develop physical manifestations of communication and transport systems to replace the psychic ones. For example in terms of travel, again people loved the fact they were able hop on an aeroplane and fly to anywhere on the planet. But this too had not been necessary in earlier times, because if one needed or wished to travel to another part of the world, they would have done this by astral travel. They would have psychically projected their minds to where they wished to go, and their consciousness would have reached the place, whilst their physical bodies remained in the original location.

Because the vibrational frequencies in the past were much finer and lighter, such travel was much easier to accomplish. Astral travel and psychic communication was seen as a normal and everyday occurrence, as mundane as traveling by car or communicating via electronic means was viewed in later times.

I noticed that with the acceleration of worldwide communication, communities that had lived in relative ignorance with regard to their material living conditions and standard of living and in many cases poverty were able to access video images of western life-styles that appeared to offer a much better life. This created a great sense of dissatisfaction in millions of people. This dissatisfaction formed part of the collective consciousness of humanity, and from a spiritual perspective, it was evident that collectively a high proportion of the human race, even those with extravagant and excessive material lives felt a pronounced level of dissatisfaction with their lives. Proof indeed, that no matter how many material possessions one had, accumulating possessions would never lead to peace of mind.

This created a sense of instability globally, not only on a collective consciousness level, but politically too. Mother Earth felt this unrest and was suffering as a result of the majority of beings failing to recognise the Great Spirit inherent in all sentient existence. Her unrest and sadness manifested in extreme weather patterns, Earthquakes, and so called "natural disasters".

The unrest in humanity manifested in increased violence, and an increased sense of separateness. Nations and communities felt divided, this was not helped by the vast difference between "rich and poor", this was becoming more and more noticeable, it was completely understandable that those in poverty sought a better life-style, and mother Earth had enough resource for everyone, the problems occurred with regard to how the resources were distributed.

During these times the world was dominated by huge corporations. The major corporations and banks held all the power, trade was rigged with the large corporations looking out for their sister companies, which served to keep out the smaller traders. Although people were seeking a life away from poverty, in reality, they exchanged one form of poverty for another. The conditions for the majority of working people were poor, there was a massive difference between the people who owned the huge business and those that worked for them. The corporations had one aim only, growth and profit, they were unconcerned about the welfare of the people who worked for them, and unconcerned about how their actions impacted on the planet.

Although those turning away from poverty to work in these conditions would perhaps be able to afford regular food and some shelter, the cost in terms of loss of spirituality and sense of pride and self-respect was not to be overlooked. They often failed to find any greater happiness in their souls, even though on the surface their material conditions appeared to have improved.

At this time most of the world leaders had been supported by election campaigns funded by the dominating corporations, any candidates not from that elk would be squeezed out and marginalised, making the chances of them being elected almost impossible. The media was also owned by the same handful of corporations, so they would ensure inaccurate propaganda was published, always to serve the end of enhancing their electoral candidate. Of course this served a very useful purpose for them, because once their candidate had been elected, they would ensure that the government policies and laws would be favourable to the continued existence of the mighty corporations, and ensured there were plenty of loopholes in tax laws that they could take advantage of, as their over-all philosophy was that the rules were for everyone else, but did not apply to them.

It seemed as though the polarities between people were at unprecedented levels, instead of a unity and coming together of communities, it appeared as though the opposite was evidential throughout the world. However, as the world appeared to be growing more and more insane, it became apparent that growing numbers of the world population were not willing to accept this as their reality.

There were small groups of enlightened people dotted all around the world, that listened to their inner-being and higher consciousness. Unwilling to listen to the popular culture or media "reality" they felt the need to reach out and give a voice to the Great Spirit and to mother Earth. These groups had varying outward identities, for example, some were small-scale environmentalists or involved in community initiatives, others included shamans, mediums, authors, gardeners, therapists, artists, yoga and meditation groups, or simply sensitive individuals who did not subscribe to any particular group or identity. The key feature all these had in common was their open hearts, wakefulness and their ability to think beyond the present cultural "norms". They also had some sort of sense and awareness of the Great Spirit, or the spirit of the Earth inherent in all living things. The world was on the cusp of change, there was growing potential for a new Earth, all it would take was for enough of these like-minded people to raise their thought vibrations and link together their collective consciousness.

If enough people were prepared to do this, then the old power paradigm would not be able to survive, and we would welcome a new Earth. An Earth where the planet was respected and honoured for the wise and loving being it truly was, where diversity and loving cooperation went hand in hand, where spiritual contemplation was a normal everyday occurrence, where people were in touch with their higher-selves, and were naturally in tune with their inner- wisdom. The message was clear, as individuals we really could make a difference, it was not time to sit around waiting for others to take action, it was not time to have a defeatist attitude, that would be just like giving up, everyone and anyone could truly make a difference. Change was affront, momentum was gathering, the anticipatory winds of change began to blow.

CHAPTER 6 – A MIRROR VIEW

The world was in flux, uncertainty was rife, yet there was an abundance of souls ready and waiting to move on to the next level of consciousness, so just how would they manage this? As stated earlier at this time mother Earth was feeling the tensions of the unrest and polarities in the collective consciousness of humanity. This was being expressed by erratic weather patterns, "natural disasters" such as floods, bush fires, Earthquakes.

From a material and humanistic perspective, the impact this phenomena was having on humans was truly devastating. People had lost their homes, their livelihoods, all the material possessions and security they had accumulated throughout their lives had been wiped out, with little chance of full recovery. On the surface those situations appeared hopeless and disastrous, however, from a spiritual perspective a whole new chapter of human history was beginning to come into play.

When humans were stripped away of their Earthly possessions, and were left with "nothing", when there were literally no material distractions left, when they had lost their cars, hobbies, electronic devices and communication systems, TV's, clothes, when there was no means of escape, when there were no worldly diversions available, where then would they turn?

For many people it was only when life reached that critical point, would they be willing to let go of the mental position that deemed matter and material possessions as the sum total of their lives. When people were living in material comfort and ease, they were less likely to seek a deeper meaning in life or any kind of spiritual purpose. If they had felt any sense of dissatisfaction at all, chances are that would have simply have motivated them to chase even more material possessions and distractions. However, a different reality was beginning to emerge, the weather systems and "natural disasters" were offering people conditions favourable to spiritual awakening, they acted as a calling card, it seemed to be saying "wake up now, or face further heartache and suffering".

It was not easy to observe world events during these times, it seemed as though the whole world was in chaos on so many different levels. There were the obvious problems with politics, world leaders pulling in opposite directions, wars and conflict, communities divided by opposing politics and community ideals. Normal everyday people were being lost to terrorism and chemical warfare. It seemed that in many parts of the world no-one trusted anyone with a different ethnicity or religious background.

There was no balance in terms of the Earth's resources, there were still large numbers of humans incarnate on Earth that were devoid of basic survival things such as clean water, food and shelter, yet on the other hand huge numbers of humans were suffering from obesity and health related problems due to over-indulgence. The natural resources of the Earth were being plundered and pillaged in the name of commerce; large de-forestation projects were rife, over-fishing was commonplace, the extraction of fossil fuels by means of fracking and drilling were sanctioned without any consideration for the environmental impact.

Disregarded plastic products were polluting the oceans and killing marine life, the development of new roads and housing were driving wildlife and nature out of their natural habitats, with ever- increasing numbers of species becoming extinct.

It was as though the whole world was whipping up a frenzied and chaotic energy. At times it was difficult to observe that madness and not get embroiled in the collective drama and anxiety. I had to make constant efforts to be in touch with my higher-self in order to not get drawn in. I was reminded of the laws of karma, and had to remind myself that there was a wisdom inherent in all of it, and that there were many beings in the world of spirit teaming together to help the Earth at that critical point.

The violent winds of change ripped through the landscapes, no-one knew what the next day would bring, be it on a political level, or with regard to the weather patterns. The only thing that was predictable was uncertainty. And yet this appeared to be driving people to pursue the next level of consciousness, they knew that there was more than the reality they were living. Many felt this on a soul level, but were not able to articulate it, or even consciously acknowledge it within their usual state of being. There was an increase in the uptake of people interested in the Eastern philosophies such as Yoga, Tai Chi, Buddhism, as well as growing numbers of people interested in common law and community projects, meditation groups and other spiritual projects. The participants of these groups were reaching out for the next level of consciousness; it was time for them to move on.

The intention to move forward spiritually was there, one of the best ways for these people to do this, would be for them to access their higher-selves. As a graduate of Rycia, I was only too aware of how important it was to listen to the soul and have frequent contact with ones higher-self. As I knew it was the best way for someone to stay connected with their life-purpose, and keep them on the spiritual path they had chosen prior to birth, during the life-plan stage.

So far this story has mentioned the concept of a life review; usually soon after death, when the soul was ready, it would have the opportunity to undertake a life-review. This was where along with its main spirit guide/guardian angel, it would have the chance to observe all that it has said and done during the life it has just left. There was no getting away from the truth, if for example the person having the life review had chosen to deny an aspect of its behaviour and pretend it had not happen, it would still come to light in the life-review. The main purpose of this was to help the soul to identify things it did well, things it did not do, and things it could do better, then forge some idea as to the next steps that soul needed to take in terms of its own progression. For those familiar with work-place performance reviews, it would be a bit like that, but in this case the entire life was reviewed, every aspect.

As mentioned previously, many souls lost sight of their life-plan once they were incarnated on Earth, they often went way off track, that was especially the case during times when spirituality was not interwoven into the living cultures of everyday life. When people had lost sight of their life-plans, often during the life-review they would be full of remorse or regret for opportunities wasted, and for unhelpful behaviours that would have a detrimental impact on their soul progression. They may then spend many subsequent life-times trying to work out the karma of the life they had just left.

So from this point of view, being able to tune into the higher-self whilst still in incarnation, almost be like having the benefit of hindsight. As being able to connect with one's higher-self, gave the chance to check-in with oneself, recognise if one had begun to go off track. If so would afford time to put in some strategies to bring about behaviours that were more akin to the life-plan and soul progression plan, rather than having a life-style moving in the opposite direction to that which one had planned.

Something that helped people connect with their higher selves was engagement in yoga, meditation and mindfulness practice. There were growing numbers of "ordinary" people turning to these spiritual practices, and I observed lots of hype around about mindfulness. It was being branded as a "new" concept, some even attempted to take ownership of it, and stated that unless you had engaged with their own particular training, it was unsafe to practice. When in fact the idea of mindfulness, that was to be able to quieten the mind, to observe the present moment, without judgement. Notice any thought that might pass through the mind, again without judgement, and return the consciousness to the here and now. This was in fact an ancient Eastern practice, that the Buddhists had been practising for thousands of years, in this cycle of Earth existence, let alone previous times when people were naturally connected to their spiritual selves.

It was good to see that there were communities of people ready to move on to the next stage of consciousness, they wanted to connect with their souls, recognise their life-plans and live life true to themselves. They did this by attuning to their higher selves, this in itself brought about many profound changes for individuals.

Many people were familiar with the concept of an epiphany, and would relate that to a strong religious experience. However, it really was possible for everyone to experience an epiphany. All one needed to do was to open oneself to the Great Spirit, to quieten the mind, and allow the beautiful energy of the Great Spirit to flow through ones consciousness, feel a connection with the Great Spirit, and honour the life essence that is present in every living thing, and indeed the Earth itself.

Once one had experienced this phenomena, it was indeed life changing, because once open to the concept of a reality greater than the immediate existence, it was like opening the door to a completely new beautiful, wonderful world. This in itself often engendered profound change in individuals, because once opened to the Great Spirit there came an increased sense of personal responsibility, and a natural empathy with nature, and all other living beings ensued.

There was a huge shift in the mindset of the population, for exmaple growing numbers of people became interested in permaculture, electroculture and alternative ethical methods of food production. The "celebrity" cultures, media and "reality" TV began to seem insignificant, fake and pointless when compared to the reality of all that is. There was an awakening to the realisation of true inner-beauty, rather than the obsession with outward appearance and image.

Many people began to realise that their lives henceforth had been blinkered, they realised that most of the things they had previously seen as so very important and necessary were actually fake and phoney, they realised that many of their choices concerning their previous paradigm of thought, had been heavily influenced by media and the popular culture.

Having had an awareness of spiritual truth, people were naturally waking up to a new level of consciousness, shedding old behavioural and thinking patterns, this felt authentic and liberating. However, there were still those heavily invested in materialism and mammon. Despite the catastrophic changes to their material living conditions they still clung reverently to the old ways, venomously defending their positions by pouring scorn on the new ways, clinging to capitalism and commerce, and anything mainstream media told them.

The enlightened ones knew that it was pointless attempting to "convert" anyone to the new ways, as they knew that for true change to take place, a soul needed to be ready, and when they were ready they would find the truth, without anyone having to persuade them or cajole them into it. For many this was perhaps the most difficult part of the process, when part of the family awakened and became enlightened, it was difficult to watch loved ones unwilling to take that step forward to liberation and upsetting to watch their suffering, which was more than likely due to them clinging on to materialism and conforming to media expectations, whilst ignoring their inner wisdom, and spiritual selves. Never the less all the enlightened ones could do was to observe their loved ones suffer, trapped in their mistaken values and behaviours, and wait ready to extend help and assistance if it was needed.
As more and more people moved towards a more spiritual way of being, the collective consciousness began to gather momentum, instead of these groups of people being in the minority gradually the balance began to tip. This had a profound impact on the vibrational level of the planet.

Some of the major power holders such as the large corporations, banks, prominent politicians, and powerful families linked to government and mafia began to gradually lose their grip on the power-monopolies, and many of these institutions, systems and empires began to crumble and break down. This was because as people became enlightened they naturally stopped seeking the products and life-styles the old institutions told them they needed.

As part of the awakening process, people began to stop investing as much power or authority with these figures. Those institutions could only remain powerful whilst ever people thought they need something from them, esteemed them, or were fearful of them. If the majority of the masses thought of them as being inconsequential, then that deemed them a whole lot less powerful. If a circus performer loses its audience, eventually it will stop performing.

One thing I observed was that instead of allowing themselves to be dominated by powerful systems, as people became enlightened they began to step into their own personal power more readily. Not in a domineering or aggressive way, but more in terms of having respect for self, and for taking personal responsibility for their actions. In the old system, if something went wrong or not to plan, people would look for someone to blame, to pin responsibility on, and everyone wanted to get revenge or compensation. Of course, this in turn reinforced the old systems of power, and was actually keeping the masses dis-empowered. But in the new scheme of things if something did not go to plan, people simply accepted their own part in it, and did not go rushing to find a scape-goat or a compensation lawyer.

As I observed with a sense of satisfaction the demise of the old system and the new philosophical paradigm emerge, I realised that I had the pangs of homesickness for my home planet Rycia. I found this a little disconcerting, I had committed to the task of guiding humanity many eons ago, I felt guilty that I was perhaps veering from my path. I felt I was letting myself down and perhaps was not up to the job.

As always when I needed some clarification and guidance I tuned in to my higher-self and asked for guidance. My spiritual guides and masters drew close, and proposed a sort of council meeting, where we all sat in a big circle. I had to quell a sense of anxiety, as my initial thought was that I was going to have to answer questions about my ability to complete the task, given my feelings of home-sickness. However, I need not have worried, as I was met with an outpouring of love and appreciation, and it was acknowledged that the task assigned to me of over-seeing the development of the consciousness of the Earth dwellers had in fact been much more complex than had been anticipated.

I received recognition for my continued efforts throughout the many phases of Earth existence, and it was agreed that since the Earth was now ready for the next dimension to come forth, at the end of my present incarnation, my responsibility for over-seeing the Earth would be complete. An overwhelming rush of excitement and relief washed over me, although I would miss my beloved Earth, I knew it was time to move on. They told me that I still had some work to do on Earth before my transition, mainly that I needed to tell my story, because doing so would help to quell the anxieties around the seemingly catastrophic changes taking place on Earth. I was also told that human consciousness was once again ready to accept the concept of the existence of beings from other planetary systems, and that writing about Rycia and my experiences would open this up in a non-threatening way and would help open people's minds to these possibilities.

At first I found the idea of writing daunting, I had always enjoyed writing poetry but was dyslexic, had a demanding full time job, a house and family to look after, where on Earth would I find the time to write? Once again, I consulted my higher-self through meditation, and was reminded that the concept of "time" was not all it seemed and was assured that this final task was well within my capability.

I had a sense that my transition would take place when I was around seventy six years of age, therefore I had around thirty years of Earth time left. I was determined to make best use of the time left, so I simply held the faith that they were right, so in addition to all of my Earthly demands and responsibilities began to write. During the writing process, I was aware that much of the knowledge was coming from my higher-self, as well as from my spirit guides. I even consulted with the local elementals, to ensure that I was painting a reasonably accurate picture. The elementals were generous and helpful, they were glad to have their story told. It was a true honour for me to re-connect with the elementals in this way. In the end I wrote six books that were published within my own rights, and several other co-authored books.
I had a very sudden, but peaceful passing; my transition back to the spirit world was beautiful and uplifting. I promptly went through my life-review, this was relatively unremarkable. Thankfully there were no skeletons in my cupboard I needed to deal with, as I had been very mindful in this last incarnation not to incur any negative karma that would necessitate working out, but still it was a relief to have this confirmed.

Following this I knew I was free to go home. I bid a fond farewell to the Earth Masters, and to Mother Earth herself, gave my heart-felt thanks to all the beings that had helped me on my Earth journey throughout the eons of time, and set my intention for home. In terms of Earth time I had been gone for millions of light years, yet I knew that in the Rycian time-frame it was merely as though I had taken a mini-break.

Gillian England

MYSTIC HEALING THERAPIES

Gillian England

MYSTIC HEALING THERAPIES

My name is Gillian I live in England, I am a natural mystic, healer, author, psychotherapist, spiritual teacher and energy director.

My mission is to assist in the developing consciousness of the human race, as well as to bring in divine energy codes to the planet.

A graduate of the University of Derby, I have worked as a psychotherapist for over 20 years. Prior to that I was a Butlin's red coat, professional dancer and fire-eater. My heartfelt desire is to help people help themselves, by assisting them to step into their divine power. Sometimes people need a little assistance, be it releasing them from prior contracts, spells, entity attachments, or connecting them to their star heritage or higher selves. Mystic Healing Therapies can be the gateway to this, I will see you, and honour your experience, whatever that might be.

www.gillianengland.com

You can also find me on youtube and telegram

Gillian England
MYSTIC HEALING THERAPIES

Also available as part of the 'Road to Enchantment Series' is BOOK TWO 'Spiritual Development in 5D'

www.gillianengland.com

Printed in Great Britain
by Amazon